QuietSpacing®

Second Edition

**A Guide to Regaining
Command of Your Day,
Getting More Done, and
Enjoying Greater Satisfaction**

Revised and Updated
Includes Free Online Demo Library
Uses Microsoft Outlook 2010 in Application

PAUL H. BURTON

QuietSpacing®

A Guide to Regaining Command of Your Day, Getting More Done, and Enjoying Greater Satisfaction

Second Edition

Copyright © 2012 by Paul H. Burton

Published by:
Paul H. Burton
www.quietspacing.com

Page layout by Ad Graphics, Inc., Tulsa, OK 74145

Printed in the United States of America

ISBN 978-0-9818911-3-2

Dedication

To my clients: may each of you benefit
from our time together as much as I do.

About Paul H. Burton

Paul H. Burton is a former attorney, software executive, and successful entrepreneur. He helps clients regain command of their day, get more done, and enjoy greater personal and professional satisfaction. Paul is available for keynote presentations, interactive training seminars, and individualized coaching services. You can learn more about Paul and his work at www.quietspacing.com.

TABLE OF CONTENTS

Chapter 1

The Always-Connected World

*QuietSpacing® can produce impressive results. In early 2006, a client asked me to work with one of their young up-and-coming professionals whose personal life had recently become tumultuous, resulting in lowered job performance. Working with her was very fruitful, as she truly wanted to regain control of her professional and personal lives. Implementing the QuietSpacing® method resulted in an increase of nearly **100 additional measured hours** of productivity over nine months! More important, she felt like she was in charge of her career and her home life again, as well as in command of her work instead of enslaved by it.*

Is *frantically frenetic* redundant? Maybe—but it nonetheless succinctly describes the modern workday. Peter Drucker's "knowledge workers" have become victims of near-constant interruption and distraction. Whether it's the ping of new e-mails hitting your Inbox, the squawk of your phone notifying you of a new call, or the vibration of your BlackBerry across your desk, your day reverberates with sound. Added to the external mayhem is the persistent inner voice reminding you of what must get done: "Gotta do this ..." "Gotta do that ..." "Oh yeah, gotta do that thing too." Never mind the cacophony that clients, colleagues, and coworkers add to the mix. All this *stuff* produces a deafening amount of *noise*.

The result of this clamor is reduced productivity, marginalized responsiveness, and lowered effectiveness, accompanied by increased stress and dissatisfaction. The more mired in the noise you become, the less you get done and the more the pressure mounts. In the end, you feel overwhelmed and unfulfilled. Is that really how you want to spend your time at work?

The Culprit

Technology is the culprit, of course. Desktops, laptops, and mobile devices deliver a constant flow of e-mails, documents, spam, requests, and to-dos of every stripe over high-speed and wireless networks twenty-four hours a day. It is all part of the symphony of modern life.

The problem, though, lies not with the technology itself but with how we integrate it into our lives. Technology does nothing we don't ask of it. It is merely a tool we can use productively or wastefully, just like the processes surrounding it. Because technology changes so rapidly, we mere mortals tend to lag behind in harnessing its value. As a result, we become enslaved by it, never quite finding the time to master the functions or properly integrate the available tools into a productive workflow-management system.

A Solution to the Quandary

Enter QuietSpacing®—a revolutionary way to manage the flow of information relentlessly bombarding you and facilitate your daily productivity. QuietSpacing® increases productivity using these four steps:

- **The architecture.** Chapter 2 describes a new, simplified workflow-management model that reduces the noise in your day. It provides solutions that leverage your physical and electronic tools so you can get a better handle on your stuff.

- **The setup and implementation.** Now that you have a new understanding of how simple workflow really is and the best way to manage it, chapters 3–7 provide you with step-by-step instructions on how to set up and use the QuietSpacing® method in each of the four focal areas covered in this guide:

  - E-mail
  - Scheduling and Meetings
  - Tasks and Projects
  - Workspace

- **The QuickStart Card.** Most of the best ideas for QuietSpacing® come from my clients. The QuickStart Card included in this book is proof. It is a quick reference that you can use when you are sitting at your desk in the middle of the day. A peek at the front page reminds you of the QuietSpacing® architecture. The inside pages describe the setup steps in Microsoft Outlook 2010 that will get your software ready to power-process your daily deluge of information. Finally, the back page explains how QuietSpacing reminders work to get you on top of everything you have to do.

- **Appendix A—Five-Day Implementation Schedule.** Some students of QuietSpacing® prefer to walk before they run. Appendix A sets out a five-day schedule over which you can adopt the principles in this guide. A slower implementation schedule allows you to customize the methodology to your liking as you work through the various steps.

Return on Investment

Here's some quick math to demonstrate what a little extra quiet can mean for you.

If you capture just six additional minutes of productivity each workday, the aggregate effect is impressive:

$$
\begin{array}{r}
\textbf{6 minutes/day} \\
\times \quad \textbf{5 days/week} \\
\times \quad \textbf{48 workweeks/year} \\
\hline
\textbf{24 additional hours/year}
\end{array}
$$

That's **three days** of increased productivity. Imagine how you would feel if you had three days of work off your desk right now! Think of how much less stress you would be feeling and how much greater your command over your workload would be! Silence is indeed golden.

> ➤ **Practice Tip:** Remember that each captured six-minute increment results in three days of work off your desk ... **per year!**

QuietSpacing® Philosophy

All the math in the world may not be enough incentive for you to make the changes necessary to achieve the results promised here. Here's a simpler reason to adopt QuietSpacing®: Success is a feeling, not a result. We feel successful when we accomplish things. And to take this one step further, we use memories—snapshots in time—to record those successes. Thus, a happy, successful life is one filled with making good use of the time you have.

QuietSpacing® Tenets

The foundation of QuietSpacing® is constructed on three simple pillars. These tenets have been carefully articulated to offer an elegant framework through which you can improve your performance, gain greater control, and increase your sense of satisfaction in your chosen field.

However, a word of caution is advisable here. Understand that performance and balance are results achieved; they are not given. To reach the goals of this program, you need a compelling reason to change your behavior. That's what the math above is meant to do. Another factor critical to success is the ease with which you can adopt and maintain the new behaviors. Accordingly, take a moment to carefully consider the tenets listed below. Then, when working through the QuietSpacing® program and the related exercises in this guide, look for how you are integrating one or more of the tenets into your world.

- **Productivity is about focus.** What do you do when you *really* need to get something done? Most people close their door, turn off their phone, or go to a completely different work area. That's because they need to **focus** on the work at hand. Today's working environments are littered with interruptions and distractions. Thus, people are forced to take extreme measures (and, often, behave unprofessionally) to accomplish the immediate priority.

  The underlying architecture of QuietSpacing® is designed to allow you to focus better on what needs doing right now. The workflow method and setup instructions described below are based on the use of reminders versus to-do lists. In addition, the tips and tricks suggested throughout the focal-area chapters will reduce the number of interruptions and distractions that cripple your ability to stay focused throughout the day.

- **Stop deferring; start deciding.** Getting things done is about moving forward on tasks and projects. One of the historically bad behaviors we exhibit is deferring decisions. Note that this is different from procrastination. In fact, it's more insidious. Procrastination is actually *making* a decision to put something off—to not do it. Deferring a decision is just pushing the entire effort into the future with thoughts and statements like, "Oh, yeah. Gotta do that" and "Oops, can't forget about that."

Imagine little rubber bands attached to each of those items you push away via deferral. They represent the reminders attached to each task or project. Eventually, those deferred items are going to reach the end of their respective rubber bands and come rushing back into your head. The trouble is that we don't know how long each of those rubber bands is, so we have no control over when those reminders will come rushing back. They could come when we're working on other projects or when we're driving home or at 3:00 a.m. when we're sound asleep. Moreover, deferral behavior accomplishes nothing—and we know that in our minds. In essence, we're busy getting nothing done! Thus, every time we push something out on a rubber band, a small amount of stress and tension remains, along with the knowledge that we have yet one more thing left unattended.

By making decisions, versus deferring them, we begin to feel a sense of command over our day. Our stress level is lower, and reminders bouncing back on their rubber bands do not inter-rupt us randomly. QuietSpacing® relies on a reminder system to queue up those things that need our attention "today." The act of deciding what will be queued up for today and tomorrow and the day after tomorrow provides us with a systematic way to align the tasks and projects we are responsible for completing. It also gives us confidence that everything on our "list" has been attended to, and we can focus on what needs doing right now.

- **Adopt, Adapt, Reject.** Every aspect of QuietSpacing® was constructed through my work with clients. Consequently, each piece can stand alone or be integrated into the whole in personalized ways that work for you. When considering the suggestions in this program, work with them in this order:

  □ *Adopt:* Can you adopt a suggestion into your workflow? Try it for a day or two and see.

  □ *Adapt:* If a particular suggestion isn't fitting into your regimen, but you like the concept behind it, adopt the concept and adapt the method in a way that achieves the intended benefit.

  □ *Reject:* If you can't adopt or adapt a suggestion, reject it, and move on to the next one. You will need only one or two from the dozens included in this book to capture your six additional minutes of productivity a day.

A Test-Drive Exercise

Still skeptical? Try this simulation exercise: Turn off your computer monitor and smartphone, put your office phone on Do Not Disturb, close your door, and move all the files and other piles off your desk (preferably out of sight). Now, take one file, place it on your desk, and work on it for thirty minutes or until you have completed the next step in that project. Go ahead. I'll wait …

Pretty amazing what you just accomplished in that brief time, eh? Establishing a focused environment devoid of interruptions and distractions does wonders for your productivity and sense of accomplishment.

Now, let's get into the details of the QuietSpacing® program so you can accomplish even more!

Chapter 2

The QuietSpacing® Architecture

Working with successful people is a privilege for me. My clients are bright, hardworking, capable individuals who are constantly striving to improve themselves and those around them. The work has its lighter sides too. Once, I was coaching a senior executive of a midsized professional-services firm in the Pacific Northwest. After going through the QuietSpacing® architecture drill, he commented that he couldn't believe they were paying me to point out such obvious things. My response? That elegance—the intersection of form and function—is always obvious once achieved! Nary an invoice to them went past due. ...

The following describes a systematic approach to greater pro-ductivity that arose through my own experience as well as the experiences of my clients. Many of the suggestions can be sepa-rately implemented, but the greatest benefit is achieved when you interlace your individual habits with the methods described below.

The Modern Workflow Environment

When it came time to formalize QuietSpacing®, my first task was to investigate other methods already available to people. After all, if my system isn't different—and, ideally, better—what's your motiva-tion for learning it?

I researched a number of other time-management systems and workflow theories. Most of them offered useful and effective advice. However, the one thing that was evident in all of them was that their underlying architecture, the underpinnings, was based on a working environment that no longer exists. The days when mail came only once a day, message slips were handed from assistant to boss, and meetings were primarily held face-to-face in the same office are gone. The ad-vent of the Internet and the technologies that leverage its breadth and scope have greatly expanded the "where" and "how" of our work world.

As a consequence, the time-management systems developed in bygone eras were largely ineffective at handling the near-constant stream of inputs and communications the modern worker handles every day. A new workflow architecture was needed. We needed a better way to address the amount of information coming at us in the workplace.

QuietSpacing® is that system. Its architecture is intentionally simple and easy to learn. That's because we no longer have time to ruminate about the inputs or the process we are using. When managing our workload, we need to quickly and decisively identify what any one item is and get it processed so we can get back to the immediate demands of the day. The following is a discussion of a new, highly effective way to process all that information. (Note: The front cover of the QuickStart Card included with this book is a visual representation of the QuietSpacing® workflow architecture.)

Three Steps to Workflow

"What am I doing?" That's the question we must ask ourselves first and most often when dealing with our workload. Whether it's looking at the most recent batch of e-mail that's arrived in your inbox or the files stacked up on and around your desk, understanding what you are doing right this minute is crucially important to remaining in command of your workload. It's also the seminal question in the QuietSpacing® architecture, to which there are only three answers—Gather, Assess, and Produce (GAP for short).

Let's take a closer look at each step to better understand how each plays a role in getting things done:

- **Gather.** As the first step in managing workflow, it's ironic that this is primarily a passive one. Gathering occurs, whether we are there or not. The only real effect we have on the gathering step is in where things are gathered. A good way to visualize this step is to gather everything together that's heaped up in your inbox or on the credenza in your office. That way, when we do the next step, you'll see how dramatic the change can be.

> ➤ **Practice Tip:** *Take your intra-office and USPS mail. My guess is that you have a place where you allow those things to gather—into an inbox on your desk, on the seat of your office chair, at your assistant's workstation. In fact, many people allow physical things to gather in all these spots, which makes assessing them—the next step—more difficult. Thus, with respect to our physical inputs such as files, papers, messages, and mail, the best thing we can do is create a* **single point of collection** *to gather everything. A single inbox is most effective, especially one that isn't right on your desk. That can cause unnecessary distraction whenever someone enters to place something in it. In fact, inboxes are most useful when placed near the door or at an assistant's workstation. Fortunately, e-mail is generally gathered in one spot—the inbox—so we don't have to worry too much about that at this point.*

- **Assess.** Once everything is gathered, the next step in the QuietSpacing® workflow model is to assess each item. Basically, we are looking to identify what category the stuff in front of us falls into and, if it's Work, what type of Work it is. (Identifying Work types is discussed in the next section.) The point here is to understand that assessing what is gathered is a specific step in workflow management. Many people treat the assess step in an as-needed or reactive manner, which causes them to bounce from one thing to the next without ever really moving the ball down the field. By asking, "What am I doing?" we retake command of the process, specifically the assess step, allowing us to more effectively process our Work.

> ➤ **Practice Tip:** *You must understand and embrace the administrative nature of the assess step. Whenever you are assessing your inputs, you are not producing (the next step). This is inherently true, and it costs you time. The question you need to ask is whether a formal assessment process during which you are aware of the administrative time you are expending is more efficient and effective than a haphazard process where you ping-pong between production and assessment with little or no awareness of the administrative time you are expending. My experience is that a methodical approach is more effective and efficient, but that is something everyone has to determine for themselves.*

- **Produce.** With all the gathered stuff assessed, we can get back to work—the production part of our day. This is the place where we want to spend as much time as possible every day. The most effective way to do that is to (a) have an effective way of managing our inputs (i.e., the previous two steps) and (b) reduce the number of interruptions and distractions that we suffer each day and that reduce our productive time. The chapters to come are each preceded by a series of QuickTips that are offered as ways to minimize those interruptions and distractions that inhibit production time.

That's it; that's what we do each day. The graphic used to represent the GAP workflow process is intentionally circular to represent that the process of Gathering, Assessing, and Producing is never ending. We do it every day and throughout each day. Remember, the key to successfully leveraging the QuietSpacing® method is to regularly ask yourself, "What am I doing?"

Categorizing Stuff

With the high-level architecture in place, we can drill down to the heart of the assess step. QuietSpacing® is fundamentally a workflow-processing engine. It provides a construct for identifying where we are in terms of our workflow, a categorization mechanism for quickly sorting the inputs we receive, and a reminder system for systematically queuing up those items that need our attention. We've looked at the first step of the QuietSpacing® construct; now, let's turn to the categorization mechanism.

"What is this?" That's the question that categorizes all the stuff—physical and electronic—you deal with in the course of your day. All stuff can be put into one of four categories:

- **Trash.** Trash is all the stuff you no longer need. It can be re-moved from your life entirely. Rarely does the struggle lie in identifying Trash; it's usually in mustering the courage to dis-card the stuff.

- **Archive.** This is stuff you no longer need at your fingertips but may need to see again later. Like Trash, Archive stuff can leave your present world. Again, identifying Archive stuff is easy. Getting it out of sight is harder.

> ➤ **Practice Tip:** Everything in your office that you won't be touching in the next two weeks is in the Archive category. We'll be moving these materials out of your office and using a reminder sys-tem to make sure you don't forget about them.

- **Reference.** You need certain materials on hand for periodic reference. For example, many people use form books, directories, and the like regularly in the course of their day. Handling Reference materials is a process issue.

- **Work.** Work is **anything that must get done**. For example, preparing for a meeting is Work. So is doing an employee review and going grocery shopping. Sending a memo is Work, as is picking up the kids from day care.

That's all there is. Really—just four types of stuff. (Let me know if you find a fifth!)

The State of Stuff

This may be obvious, but stuff exists in only two states—Open or Closed.

- **Open.** Open stuff is anything that has yet to be completed. Work is the only type of Open stuff. And before you go seeking a refund on your seminar or this guide, understand that many of my coaching clients struggle with this very issue. The watershed moment for many comes when they realize that much of what surrounds them is really not Open stuff.

- **Closed.** Closed stuff is anything that is completed. Trash, Archive, and Reference are all this kind of stuff. Once categorized as Closed, this stuff can be removed from the working environment. This is discussed in detail in the next section.

Whenever something is difficult to place in one of the four categories of stuff listed above, simply ask, "Does anything further need to be done on this item?" If the answer is yes, the item is Open and, by definition, Work. If the answer is no, then it's Closed and must necessarily be Trash, Archive, or Reference.

Processing Our Stuff

All stuff must be processed and managed. The difference between QuietSpacing® and other workflow or time-management systems is that the focus of QuietSpacing® is on simplicity, the simplicity needed to effect efficiency and peace of mind.

Thus, assessing our stuff is like the triage process medical professionals use to determine which injured person gets attention first, second, and third. The objective is to quickly identify what category each item falls into, then immediately dispatch it based on that categorization. The following image gives us a visual representation of how QuietSpacing® quickly triages our stuff:

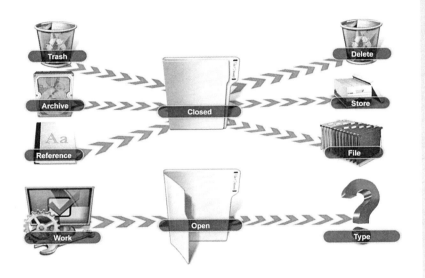

The "What is it?" question drives both the categorization of our stuff and the next action we need to take with it. Based on the categorization you determine, you'll choose from this list of actions:

- **Trash.** This is Closed stuff. Remove it from your world by throwing it out. Just do it. Move on.

- **Archive.** This is also Closed stuff. Complete the closure process by filing it away or delegating that action to someone else—your assistant?

> ➤ **Practice Tip:** *If you are in charge of filing things into long-term storage, designate a specific time each day or week to process some of your Archive materials. Slow but steady progress on a large effort is far better than no progress at all.*

- **Reference.** This is the final type of Closed stuff. Use the same solution you did with Archive—either start a reference library (slow but sure) or delegate the task to someone else. Note: Reference filing should be closer at hand since the nature of Reference material means we use it periodically to do our work.

- **Work.** Of course, this is Open stuff. This is what needs to be done, so it takes a bit more administrative time to handle properly, which is explained in further detail below.

> ➤ **Practice Tip:** *Closed stuff must leave the workspace. I'm tenacious about this because it's been my experience that most people are horrible at this step. There appears to be a well-adopted belief that leaving piles, files, and boxes lying around is a sign of a highly productive person. The reality is that it not only leaves others with a bad impression, but also (1) creates a lot of unnecessary noise and wasted effort because of the near-constant need to move it around or rummage through it and (2) generally disguises what may be legitimate Work hidden within the disaster.*
>
> *Deal with the Closed stuff during the triage step. Get it out of your way, your sight, and your office. There are lots of simple ways to do this, including carrying the Closed stuff out to your assistant's work area (or to central filing) with instructions to file it. If that doesn't work, just place a sticky note with those instructions on the stuff, and place it in your outbox.*

Stop! Notice that once we've triaged all our stuff, the only thing left Open is Work. We have reduced the amount of stuff in our life by 75 percent—all the Trash, Archive, and Reference stuff is gone. Clients are often amazed by how "quiet" their workspace feels after they've completed their first triage. We'll talk more about that later, but consider briefly before moving on that most of the noise in our world is generated by Closed stuff!

Sorting the Different Types of Work

Once we've triaged our stuff and removed the Closed items from our inboxes or workspaces, we are ready to deal with our Work. The question we need to ask next is "What type of Work is this?" Conveniently, there are also only four types of Work, as demonstrated below:

- Action Items. This is Work that you, personally, must do—all the things that are in your court to accomplish.

> ▷ **Practice Tip:** A best practice when dealing with Action Items is to list (electronically or physically) all tasks requiring completion and organize related tasks into projects when necessary for organizational sanity.

15

- **Awaiting Response.** This is Work that you need for someone else to accomplish before you can move forward—for example, a return phone call, suggested revisions to a memo, or a scheduling question with your dentist. There's nothing directly you need to do right now, but you do need to track it.

- **Pending.** Though a little nebulous, Pending refers to Work that is waiting for a particular *event to occur or date to pass* before anything can proceed. In essence, the item is not yet ripe for action. The passage of a respond-by date is a good example of a Pending item. Someone's return from vacation is another good example. You might simply be waiting for the new instant oil change joint to open. All of these types of things are Pending. Note: Once a Pending event occurs, the Work matures into an Action Item or an Awaiting Response item.

- **Reading.** These are all the things we need to read so we can stay abreast of the latest in our chosen area of expertise or our career.

> ➤ *Practice Tip:* A fundamental distinction between Work and other types of stuff can be found in its nature. Work is in process from the time it originates until the time it is completed. For example, Work can start as an Action Item, shift into Awaiting Response, become a Pending matter, then circle back to being an Action Item before being finished and, thereby, Closed (Trash, Archive, or Reference).
>
> Other types of stuff do not exhibit this quality. The term Work in Process or WIP is often used to describe it. QuietSpacing® makes frequent use of the WIP concept when managing Work itself.

Let's conduct a quick review of what we've accomplished with the QuietSpacing® framework thus far. First, we envisioned a circular construct to denote the never-ending nature of Gathering, Assessing, and Producing that goes on during our hectic workdays. Next, we put some semblance of order into the day at the assessment stage by identifying the four categories of stuff that come at us—Trash, Archive, Reference, and Work. Noting that Trash, Archive, and Reference are all Closed items, we were left with the only Open item—Work—with which to contend. We found that all Work can be classified as one of four types—Action Items, Awaiting Response, Pending, and Reading.

As a result of processing our stuff in this manner, we have removed 75 percent of it from our workplace and are left with just the things that need doing in front of us. Not a bad day's work in and of itself!

Exercise — Conducting an Assessment

Before turning to the last element of QuietSpacing®—using reminders to queue up our Work in an effective and efficient manner—let's practice the assessment process—triage, as it were—as we understand it thus far. It's important to get a good feel for this right now.

To start the exercise, identify a defined space in your office—maybe the four corners of your desk or the top of a credenza stacked with files. Pick up each item in that space and triage it—decide whether it's Trash, Archive, Reference, or Work. When you find Closed items, get them out of your workspace. (Remember, if you can't quickly categorize an item, ask if something further needs to be done with it. If not, it's Closed and goes into one of the three Closed categories. If so, it's Open Work.) For things in the Work category, decide whether each one is an Action Item, Awaiting Response, Pending, or Reading. If you cruise through the first identified space quickly, move on to another. You'll find that the triaging process goes fast once you've memorized the QuietSpacing® architecture.

> ➤ **Practice Tip:** Take the QuickStart Card that came with this book, and cut it in half. Tape the front page to a place where you can readily see it—like the edge of your computer monitor. This page contains the entire QuietSpacing® architecture, and if you display it prominently, it will be at your fingertips as you begin using the system. (Note: The QuickStart Card is Reference stuff, and by taping it to your monitor, you have "filed" it appropriately!)

The QuietSpacing® Engine—Reminders

The heart of QuietSpacing® is its use of reminders. After we have determined what type of Work each item is, we then ask, "When do I need to think about this again?" The answer to that question is the reminder date we place on that item so it will be queued in a timely fashion.

By using reminder, we can eliminate the need to remember everything physically (via pings and piles) or mentally (as in "Oh yeah, this," and "Oh, and that too!"). This reduces the audible, visual, and mental noise, making your space *quiet*. Reminders allow us to get our Work literally out of sight, out of hearing, and out of mind. When we do this, we can focus on what needs doing right now.

- **Reminders versus to-do lists:** Most people use to-do lists to track their workload. Using reminders is different from using to-do lists in two critical ways.

  - **In-line, not stopgap.** To-do lists are functionally snapshots in time—what needed to be done at the moment you created the list. They become outdated almost immediately and require constant revision. Those revisions take time, time that could be spent actually getting things done.

    The QuietSpacing® reminder system operates more efficiently. During the assessment step of processing, everything that is identified as Work gets a reminder. The reminder date you set is a date on which you want to be "reminded" that this Work exists. (The variables that go into that decision are discussed in detail below.) Thus, you are managing your Work in the flow of the day. The first time is during the triage process. Later, when the reminder pops up, you again deal with it in the ordinary course of work versus repeatedly placing it on a list until it is completed. The time saved is better spent engaging in productive effort.

  - **Can't-forget versus forced-to-remember.** To-do lists essentially operate on a "forced-to-remember" basis. That is, the long list you produce looks out into the future and serves as a giant weight of what must get done. The defocusing effects and pressure that this imposes on you can be overwhelming.

Using reminders eliminates that pressure and allows you to focus on what needs doing right now. This distinction is self-evident to anyone who has used a docketing or tickler system. These systems operate on reminder dates you select. Once you select a date, you *forget* about the matter until the date arrives, and the system serves up the reminder. That item produces no distraction or pressure in the interim. QuietSpacing® leverages this same value by prescribing a set of reminder mechanisms employed during the triage process.

Before jumping into the specifics of the QuietSpacing® reminders, we need to establish a couple of rules for their use.

- **Rules for reminders.** There are two rules to abide by when using QuietSpacing® reminders:

  □ **Renegotiating.** QuietSpacing®'s greatest gift is the authority to renegotiate reminder dates on your Work stuff. Exercise this gift frequently.

  Reminders, by definition, are set out into the future. When setting a reminder, you have little visibility into what's going to happen between now and the date you set. Therefore, reminder dates are just guesses, although ideally, educated guesses. When you reach that future date, you'll have a much better handle on what takes priority right then.

  When a QuietSpacing® reminder pops up, you can decide to (1) deal with it or (2) renegotiate it to a future date (maybe a little closer to the present) when you want to be reminded about it again. You haven't "failed" to accomplish something; you've successfully renegotiated the reminder date!

Consider the renegotiation of reminders as a tool to facilitate your workflow. Whenever you are renegotiating one, consider the content of the reminder—the underlying substance of the Work—that's being renegotiated, and base your new reminder date on that content. In addition, make the new reminder date a little closer to the present than the last one so that you are narrowing down your execution time frame.

> ➤ **Practice Tip:** You MUST renegotiate every reminder for items that did not get completed by the end of every day! QuietSpacing® is an active management system requiring your constant input. The management time is minimal, but the payback is huge. Renegotiating reminder dates every day keeps your system (and you) current. Failure to do so is the functional equivalent of letting things pile up again.

▫ **Backsliding and recovering.** Demands on your time ebb and flow. Sometimes things are very busy, and sometimes they are relatively slow. Common QuietSpacing® occurrences are backsliding (letting the system or your behaviors slip behind) and recovery (the concerted effort to get caught up again). This is like walking up a sand dune. Sometimes your footing is good, and you make great progress. Sometimes you slide back a little with each step. But simply giving up is not an option. You have to forge ahead until you reach good footing again. As stuff ebbs and flows through your days and you find yourself drifting behind, make a concerted effort to look at what's "on the list" and renegotiate things into a more manageable flow.

> ➤ **Practice Tip:** If you are still struggling with the difference between reminders and to-do lists, think of the QuietSpacing® reminder system as a constantly cycling to-do list that updates automatically during each triaging and renegotiation period.

Types of Reminders

There are two primary types of reminders—physical and electronic. (This book assumes the use of Microsoft Outlook 2010 for electronic reminders. Other productivity suites—ACT!, Lotus Notes, and others—have similar functionality. Just Adopt, Adapt, Reject!)

> ➤ **Practice Tip:** *Part of picking the reminder date involves understanding how long the task or project will take as well as any applicable deadlines. Note too that real deadlines have dates on them—as opposed to the ASAP deadlines we most often encounter. Therefore, you will need to be both diplomatic and persistent in seeking actual calendar dates for much of the Work you will be doing.*

- **Physical reminders.** Most people use the "stacks of files" method for remembering what needs to be done. The noise that this system generates can be very distracting. I recommend you establish a two-drawer filing system that stores two weeks' worth of Work. One drawer is always "This Week," and the other drawer is always "Next Week." (You can use magnetic indicators for this, but a couple of sticky notes will do the trick too.) We will set these drawers up later in the book.

As you interact with your physical stuff, you will determine which day you want to be reminded that it *exists*. If it's in the next two weeks, you will place that stuff in the folder for the appropriate day in the two-drawer filing system (for example, Tuesday, This Week; or Thursday, Next Week). If the reminder date is outside the next two weeks, the stuff gets *archived* with a reminder to pull it on the prescribed reminder date. The net result is a much lower volume of noise in your workspace.

21

> ➤ **Practice Tip:** *There is no magic to using only two drawers—This Week and Next Week. That is used simply as an example. Some clients use as many as five drawers to track their physical workload. Note, also, that a bookshelf works as well as a filing cabinet for our purposes. The result we're seeking is to have all Work categorized, to have reminder dates assigned, and to have it moved to a common storage area for temporary storage until the reminder dates arrive.*

- **Electronic reminders.** Outlook has two great features for queuing up stuff—Reminders and Flag for Follow-up. Reminders are used with the Tasks and Calendar functions. Flag for Follow-up is used with the Inbox (for e-mail) and Contacts functions.

  ◻ **Outlook reminders.** When setting up an event in Calendar or an item in Tasks, you will notice the Reminder checkbox just above the comment area, as well as the Due Date (for tasks) and Start Time (for appointments). The key to QuietSpacing® your Tasks and Calendar is setting a reminder for everything—literally everything.

    1. *Setting calendar reminders:* In the Calendar function of Outlook, you only need to make sure the Reminder time is set so you receive the amount of advance notice you want—for example, fifteen minutes.

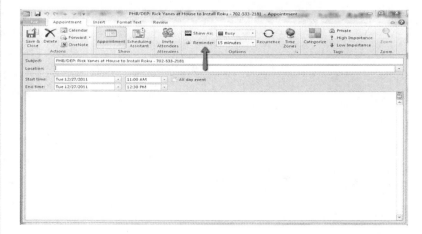

2. *Setting task reminders:* In the Task function of Microsoft Outlook, make sure the Reminder checkbox is checked, and set the Due Date *for the date that you want to be reminded that the task exists*. Disregard the Start Date; we don't use it in QuietSpacing®.

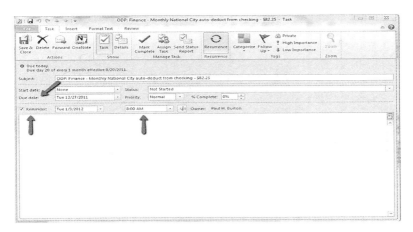

> ➤ **Practice Tip:** *Leave the Reminder start times at 8:00 a.m. This will bring all your reminders up at the beginning of each day, thus giving you a better idea of what you can get done and what you need to renegotiate. Moreover, having task reminders pop up throughout the working day only increases your noise!*

Nothing else has to be done with reminders for Tasks or Calendar items. On the appointed date, an Outlook box called the Reminders Window will pop up, listing the tasks set for that day. Calendar Appointments will pop into your Reminders Window box at the preset advanced notice time.

In addition, beginning with Outlook 2007 and continuing into Outlook 2010, Microsoft added a piece of functionality called the To-Do Bar. The To-Do Bar is a terrific addition to Outlook, as it allows us to maintain visual contact with our reminders throughout the day. A detailed discussion about the setup and use of the To-Do Bar appears below, so for right now, we simply need to be aware that we will employ it to run QuietSpacing®.

You manage reminders in Calendar differently from how you manage them in Tasks. For Calendar events, you can simply dismiss the event from the Reminders Window once it has passed. For Tasks, if the work is done, you need to mark it Complete—either from inside the task or from the Reminders Window.

1. *From the Reminders Window:* Right-click on the item and mark Complete. (This is important: Dismissing a task from the Reminders Window turns off the reminder but does not complete the task. Thus, it will still show up in the Tasks view and in the To-Do List on the To-Do Bar at the top with *no* reminder date—not a good work management practice.)

2. *From inside the task:* Select Completed in the Status drop-down box, then click Save and Close.

> ➤ **Practice Tip:** Remember, if the task is not completed by the end of the day on which the reminder was triggered, you **MUST** renegotiate it to a future reminder date.

❑ **Outlook Flag for Follow-up.** You use Flag for Follow-up to set reminders in the Inbox and Contacts functions. To set a Flag for Follow-up, open the e-mail or contact, and then click on the red flag icon in the menu bar. Set *only* the Due Date, and leave the rest of the settings alone. (The Due Date acts as our reminder engine for e-mail and contact items.)

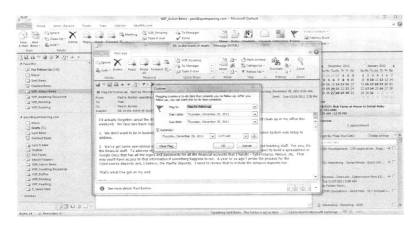

Flags operate fairly similarly to reminders. On the Due Date set for the flag to trigger, the item will appear in the To-Do Bar, as well as the list in the Tasks section of Outlook called the To-Do List. (Again, more on that below.)

1. *Using Flag for Follow-up in Contacts:* When you Flag for Follow-up a contact, it will appear in the Reminders Window pop-up box on the appointed day. Once you have completed the task related to the reminder on that contact, you need to clear the flag. Here are the steps:

   a. From the Reminders Window box: Right-click and select Clear Flag.

   b. From inside the contact: Click on the red flag icon in the menu bar and select Clear Flag.

2. *Using Flag for Follow-up with e-mail:* The most powerful use of Flag for Follow-up is with e-mail. When triaging your Inbox, you go through and flag each Work e-mail

25

to associate a reminder with that message. (We'll get into detail about what to do with these e-mails below.) Trash gets deleted. Archive and Reference items get Closed and filed by moving those messages into your long-term storage area in Outlook (or any other area dictated by your organization).

> ➤ **Practice Tip:** One more time for absolute clarity—you **MUST** renegotiate every flagged item for a future date if it did not get accomplished on the date for which it was originally flagged.

Though this system seems involved, please trust me. You'll get the hang of using these reminder types immediately once you start working with them.

Introduction to New Features in Microsoft Outlook 2010

Microsoft Office 2010 saw enhancements to many of the new features in the Outlook application first unveiled in Office 2007. This section focuses on a couple of particular features that are instrumental in making QuietSpacing® even more effective now than in its previous iterations.

- **The To-Do Bar.** The To-Do Bar is a terrific addition to Outlook. It is a customizable, vertically oriented bar that appears along the right side of the screen.

  The To-Do Bar encompasses three categories of information: Date Navigator, Appointments, and Tasks List. The Date Navigator is simply a view of one or more calendar months. The Appointments function lists a preselected number of upcoming appointments. The Tasks List expands on the Task Pad view of Outlook 2003. Grouped in the Tasks List are **all** items for which **any** kind of reminder has been set, which now includes e-mails.

To-Do Bar

This is significant because, as you'll see below, Microsoft cross-pollinated the Flag for Follow-up and Reminder functions, giving each features of the other. Functionally, it means they work very similarly to each other. Operationally, it will at first appear to be the bane of Outlook 2010 because of the possibility of being overwhelmed by a long list of reminders. However, with a little customization, the Task List in the To-Do Bar becomes a very powerful QuietSpacing® tool.

> ➤ **Practice Tip.** *Injecting the full Reminder mechanism in the Flag for Follow-up function is a benefit for QuietSpacing®. The result is that everything gets a similar style of reminder, making execution easy to learn and remember. Additionally, the expanded reminder features really fit well into the QuietSpacing® architecture, especially when combined with the To-Do Bar. The commitment you have to make is to embrace the changes and strive to see how the integration benefits your ability to put off until tomorrow that which does not need your focused attention today.*

- **Folding/Minimize panes.** Three of the view panes can now be folded out of sight or Minimized. This is a *huge* addition to the

QuietSpacing® method because out of sight *is* out of mind; more focus equals more productivity.

The three panes that can be folded are the To-Do Bar, the Navigation Pane, and in the Calendar view, the Daily Tasks List (a.k.a. Task Pad). These three panes can be set to Normal, Minimize, or Off in the View menu at the top of each screen. In addition, you can toggle between Normal and Minimize on the fly by clicking on the respective pane's chevrons. Thus, you can determine in real time what's on your screen and what isn't.

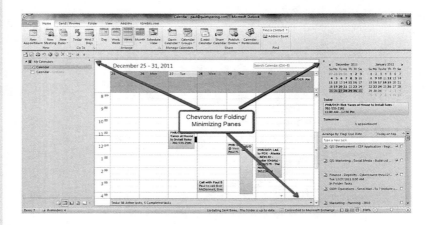

- **Expanded Flag for Follow-up and Reminder functionality.** As mentioned above, the Flag for Follow-up and Reminder functions have each been injected with their sibling's features. Now, when you open Flag for Follow-up, you'll see a virtual twin of the Calendar/Tasks reminder mechanism.

Important Note: For some reason that has not been explained, Microsoft hard-coded the reminder time in Flag for Follow-up to 4:00 p.m. This can be changed *only* manually. Note, though, that the To-Do List in the To-Do Bar will now also display those e-mails, giving you a redundant backup to ensure you remember to check them each day.

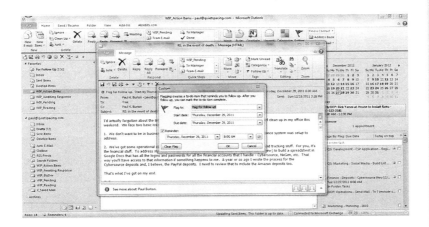

So you are faced with a choice. If you want the reminder to pop into your Reminders Window earlier, you need to manually set the time each time you set a Flag for Follow-up in an e-mail. Alternatively, you can just set the Due Date and use the To-Do List in the To-Do Bar to remind you of those things that require your attention today, tomorrow, and so on. Both work, but the latter requires less effort.

Ultimately, the good news here is that a robust and mirrored reminder system means a lot of QuietSpacing® horsepower.

Those are the most significant changes found in Outlook 2010 as they relate to QuietSpacing®. You will make many more functionality discoveries as you use the program, most of which will be realignments of existing functionality. As you become acquainted with this version of Outlook, your frustration will go down, and your effectiveness and productivity will go up.

QuickTips for E-mail

Before each focal-area chapter, a list of QuickTips related to the subject matter of that chapter is provided to help you gain some immediate time-management benefits. Here are the ones related to e-mail:

- **Turn new message notifications OFF (except the little envelope in the task tray).** E-mail is the bane of the modern world. It never stops coming! But allowing yourself to be constantly interrupted and distracted by e-mail is the equivalent of having the mail person enter your office every two minutes to drop things on your desk. The dings and beeps and vibrates and flash previews are killing you. Turn them off (*see* the QuickStart Card included with this book for instructions) and begin quieting down your space right now!

- **Triage your electronic inbox periodically—every twenty to thirty minutes or longer.** E-mail is where much of our productivity exists today. You need to check this more frequently than your physical inbox because things arrive there more often. Checking it several times an hour—versus whenever a new item appears (see turning off your notifications, above)—will suffice.

- **Include only one subject per e-mail.** The risk of confusion rises dramatically when you consolidate information about multiple subjects into a single e-mail. E-mail is essentially free to send, so reduce this risk of confusion—and its corresponding inefficiency—by including information about only a single subject in each e-mail you send.

- **Craft good Subject lines.** Whether you use a number or name or something similar, having a naming convention in the Subject line of each e-mail (and Calendar event and Tasks item) allows your recipient to read, understand, prioritize, file, and find your e-mails more rapidly. Here are some examples:

Smith/Brown: Settlement Conference—John Doe—555.333.4444

IBM/20342: Infringement Litigation—Draft Complaint—2

- **Leverage the drag-and-drop functionality.** One of the quickest ways to change an e-mail message into a Calendar event or Tasks item is to use drag and drop. Simply click on the e-mail you want to change, and drag it over the Calendar or Tasks icon, as appropriate, on the Navigation Pane (bottom left). When your cursor is hovering over that icon, "release it," and the contents of the e-mail will be copied into a new Calendar event or Tasks item. Now, all you have to do is modify the Subject line and Start and Reminder days to their appropriate settings, and you're off and running!

- **Minimize the use of Reply All.** One of the biggest boons—and banes—of e-mail is how easy it is to reply to a message and, more significantly, to "reply all" to a message. Reply All should be used sparingly to communicate substantive content that the *entire* group truly needs to know. Unfortunately, many people misuse this feature to communicate information that is really intended only for the original sender (such as acknowledging a meeting time). To remedy this problem, simply stop using Reply All unless it is really necessary. In all other circumstances, just click Reply and add back the people on the thread who need to know the information you are contributing. Doing this will reduce the amount of unnecessary e-mail passing back and forth.

Chapter 3

Power-Processing Your E-mail

Clients are often amazed at the number of "hidden" features built into Microsoft Outlook. Helping them fine-tune their Outlook setup to leverage the QuietSpacing® functionality is one of my favorite experiences. After about twenty minutes of adjustment, people get their first glimpse at how much faster and more efficient they are becoming. These realizations are usually accompanied by exclamations of "I didn't know it could do that!" and "I'm flying through these e-mails!" Their smiles at those moments are very rewarding.

E-mail is the boon and bane of the modern workplace. Most of us couldn't do our jobs effectively without it, but we also can't seem to escape it. Even when we are away from it, we know it's coming in and stacking up. The first action most people take when they get to the office is to check their e-mail, often even before grabbing their morning coffee.

Since e-mail is a necessary evil, we must seek to process it effectively, and by doing so, reduce the stress we experience as a result of this modern-day communication technology. This chapter will guide you through the process of accomplishing just that.

> ➤ **Practice Tip**. *Pull the QuickStart Card out for handy reference before you start going through the setup steps detailed below.*

Setting Up E-mail for QuietSpacing®

Remember, this book assumes the use of Microsoft Outlook 2010. The previous edition of this book covers Microsoft Outlook 2003 and 2007. Please contact us at www.quietspacing.com if you do not have the correct edition for your version of Outlook.

If you use a different productivity suite (ACT!, Groupwise, or the like), apply the Adopt, Adapt, Reject tenet from chapter 2.

OUTLOOK TODAY SETUP

Before jumping into the e-mail side of Outlook, we need to take a moment to discuss and set up a few supporting pieces of functionality: Outlook Today, the To-Do Bar, and the QuickAccess Bar.

Outlook Today is one of the best features of Outlook. It is also one that most people turn off (or that has been turned off for them) when they first load Outlook onto their computers.

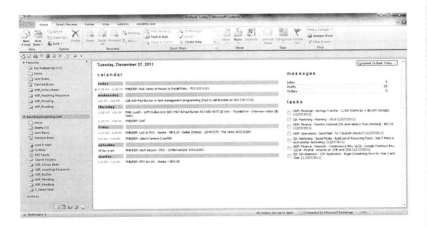

You can set this screen to be the first one that appears when you open Outlook. That way, you can see seven days of the Calendar and all the Tasks with reminders you've set for today. This gives you a terrific feel for what's going on, which is especially helpful when you are scheduling more work and meetings throughout the day. Here's what you need to do:

- **Set to open on Outlook Today.** Click on View, and make sure you have the Navigation Pane set to Normal. Enter your Inbox. Click on Personal Folders or Mailbox—[Your Name] (for Exchange users) in the Navigation Pane. That will display Outlook Today. Click on Customize Outlook Today in the top right-hand corner. Make sure "When starting, go directly to Outlook Today" is selected.

- **Customizing Outlook Today.** While still in the customization screen, select Inbox in Choose Folders under Messages. Next, select 7 days in Calendar and select Today's Tasks in Tasks (with the Include Tasks w/no Due Date box checked). As for the Styles, Two-Column or Summer seem to work best. Select Save Changes to close.

- **Getting back to Outlook Today.** If you want to get back to Outlook Today at anytime during the day, just click on Personal Folders or Mailbox—[Your Name], as appropriate, from the Inbox, and it will appear.

  Online Resource: Check out the screencast titled "Setting Up Outlook Today" for further assistance at http://www. quietspacing.com/demos.

To-Do Bar Setup

Like Outlook Today, the To-Do Bar has a life of its own. It is available in every subfunction of Outlook. Thus, whether you are viewing your e-mail, your calendar, or your tasks, the To-Do Bar is readily available for reference. The specific setup instructions below provide the quietest space while leaving ready access to this feature of Outlook.

- **Date Navigator.** This is similar to the Outlook 2003 Calendar that appeared when using the Task Pad in the Calendar view.

  To set it up, click on View at the top of the screen, and then select To-Do Bar from the ribbon. Select Options and confirm that Show Date Navigator is checked, and add 1 in the open box. This maximizes the vertical room for the To-Do List at the bottom while still providing some view into the future.

- **Appointments.** Under Show Date Navigator, confirm that Show Appointments is checked, as well as the two sub-boxes below it—Show All Day Events and Show Details of Private Items.

❏ **To-Do List.** This is a replacement function from Outlook 2003. Here's the best setup for the To-Do List:

♦ Click on the Arrange By column header, and select Show in Groups.

♦ Click on the Arrange By column header (again), and select Due Date.

♦ Click on the Arrange By column header (a third time), and select View Settings.

♦ In View Settings, click on Columns.

♦ In the drop-down titled "Maximum number of lines in compact mode," select 3.

♦ Under Available Fields, scroll down until you see Icon. Highlight it and click Add. Do the same for Complete.

♦ If Reminder Time is not already in "Show these fields in this order," then above Available Fields, click on the drop-down menu, and select Time/Info. Then select Reminder Time in the Available Fields, and click Add.

♦ In the right-hand box titled "Show these fields in this order," remove Flag Status, Due Date, Start Date, and Categories.

♦ Using the Move Up and Move Down buttons, organize the remaining items in this order:
Icon
Tasks Subject
Reminder Time
In Folder
Reminder
Complete

♦ Click OK and OK. Make sure you have selected Arranged by: Due Date and that you are sorting by Today on Top.

These may seem like tedious steps, but once you get them implemented, your entire To-Do Bar should look like this:

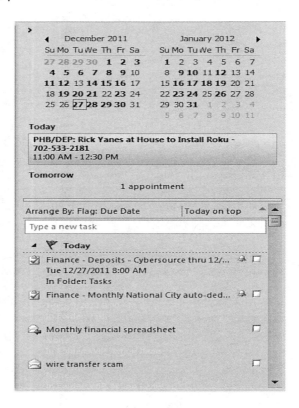

> **▶ Practice Tip.** *You can expand the size of the To-Do Bar horizontally by clicking and dragging on the border between it and the subfunction of Outlook that you are currently viewing. This resizing will remain in effect regardless of which subfunction you view.*
>
> *Online Resource: Check out the screencast titled "Setting Up the To-Do Bar" for further assistance at http://www.quietspacing.com/demos.*

We'll start seeing the To-Do Bar in action below once we get some e-mail triaged.

INBOX SETUP

Ahh, the hallowed Inbox—the place of fear and hope for every user: What will we find there this time?

The Inbox is definitely one of the noisiest stuff producers in your life, but that's going to change! The goal here is nothing less than getting your Inbox empty. That's right, *zero* e-mails in your Inbox! Imagine how quiet that is …

We'll talk about how to attain and maintain that feat later—without forgetting a single thing. Right now, we have to set up the system that accomplishes it. Here's the drill. Click on Inbox and do the following:

- **Turn off Show in Groups.** Click on View, then the little drop-down carrot for More—$\boxed{\div}$—and uncheck Show in Groups. This will eliminate the arbitrary Outlook preset of showing your e-mail by day received. We want a single list.

- **Turn off Reading Pane.** Having the Reading Pane turned on is distracting. We're setting up a handling mechanism, so distractions are *not* welcome. Click on View, Reading Pane, then Off. Don't worry, a future step delivers the same functionality as the Reading Pane but in a more efficient manner.

- **Turn off AutoPreview.** Getting just a smidgen of the e-mail to preview is simply too tempting. Turning it off forces us to triage everything in a uniform manner, which increases both efficiency and productivity. Moreover, the main objective in the Inbox setup is to gain as much visual real estate on the screen as possible. Turning off AutoPreview buys a *lot* of real estate, just as turning off the Reading Pane did. Select View, Current View, and Compact.

- **Open Next/Previous Item.** Click on File, then Options, and select Mail in the vertical list. Scroll to the very bottom and under Other, Open Next Item or Open Previous Item, depending on whether you (a) read your e-mail from the top down (Open Next Item) or (b) read your e-mail from the bottom up (Open Previous Item). Then select OK.

- **Turn New E-mail Notification off.** Click on File, Options, and Mail again. Scroll down to Message Arrival, and *unselect* Play a Sound, Briefly Change The Mouse Pointer, and Display A Desktop Alert. Leave the third item selected (Show An Envelope Icon In The Taskbar). Then select OK. This will eliminate the "ping" and flashing preview whenever a new e-mail hits your Inbox, thereby eliminating those unnecessary distractions. However, the envelope icon will appear in the bottom right of your screen (across from the Start button) whenever you have unread mail in your Inbox, so you will still be reminded to review it periodically.

- **Add To column to Inbox.** Do this step if you do *not* have the To column currently visible in your main Inbox area (the area that holds your e-mails). Right-click on any of the gray column headings in the main Inbox area (From, Subject, and so on). Select Field Chooser in the drop-down menu that appears. Scroll down to To, and drag and drop that item just to the right of From in your Inbox. (This allows you to sort items by To, which can be helpful in numerous ways as explained below.)

- **Add Due Date Column to Inbox.** Repeat the steps described in the last item above. Once you are in the Field Chooser screen, scroll down to Due Date and drag and drop that item just to the left of Received. (This allows you to sort items by Due Date, which will be useful once we start using reminders on our e-mail as explained below.)

Online Resource: Check out the screencast titled "Initial Inbox Setup" for further assistance at http://www.quietspacing.com/ demos.

ONBOARD TOOLS IN E-MAIL

Each e-mail contains all the onboard tools you need—in the form of icons in the navigation area at the top of the message—to effectively process it without having to return to the Inbox after reading it. Here's a discussion of how each function works when you click the icon associated with the function:

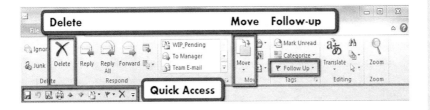

- **Delete.** Most people are familiar with the Delete function—it deletes the e-mail. (More accurately, it moves the e-mail to your Deleted folder to be disposed of in accordance with your settings regarding the long-term disposition of deleted messages.) Clicking the Delete icon in a message will, of course, delete that message. However, because of the settings changes made above, whenever you click the Delete icon now, you will (a) delete this message, *plus* (b) open the next message! As promised, no more returning to the Inbox after reviewing each e-mail. You'll be able to delete the current message you are viewing and immediately jump right into the next message. Very efficient indeed.

- **Move to Folder.** This is one of the best functions in Outlook. Clicking on this icon right inside the message gives you the opportunity to file this message in either an Outlook folder/ sub-folder or in any document-management software your organization uses.

> ➤ *Practice Tip.* *The Reading Pane is unnecessary when Outlook is set up to automatically open e-mail messages in succession.*

Whenever you are triaging e-mail and come upon something that is Archive or Reference, you can click on the Move to Folder icon. A list of the last ten folders you have used pops up, along with a link at the bottom (rather inartfully named Move to Folder, again) that will open a screen displaying all your folders. Here's what that looks like:

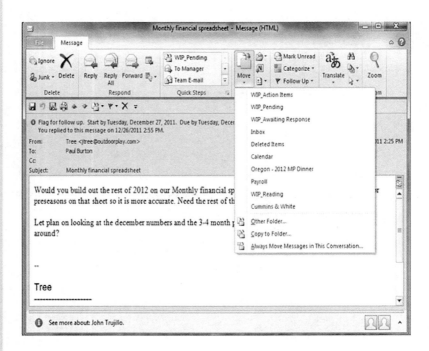

The benefit of doing this right from inside the e-mail is that as soon as you select which folder you want to file this e-mail in (or create a new folder for it), Outlook files the e-mail and *immediately opens the next message*! Together with the Delete function, you can remove your Trash, Archive, and Reference items from your Inbox as you move through a batch of e-mail. The result is that only Work is left in your Inbox, which you can manage using the Flag for Follow-up function discussed next.

- **Flag for Follow-up.** The use of Flag for Follow-up was covered under the Reminder section of the last chapter. Specifically, review the **Expanded Flag for Follow-up and Reminder functionality** bullet in chapter 2 for a detailed explanation of this function. Note: This is the *single most important* function the QuietSpacing® method relies on to power-process your e-mail. Flagging for Follow-up is a way to set reminders on individual messages so that they can be sorted according to their Due Date (a.k.a. reminder date) and be queued up in a systematic and effective manner. Please make sure you have a solid understanding of this particular function before proceeding.

> ➤ **Practice Tip.** Another time-saver is to right-click on any attachment in an e-mail and use the Save As option to quickly save just the attachment to the folder of your choice.

QUICKACCESS BAR WITHIN E-MAIL

All of the functions described above (and more) can be grouped together and made readily available through a nifty bit of functionality first introduced in Outlook 2007 called the QuickAccess Bar. To get the QuickAccess Bar set up for QuietSpacing® e-mail, follow these steps:

- **Open up an e-mail.** The QuickAccess Bar can be set for Outlook in general and for each e-mail in particular. We're looking to set it up for *e-mail*, so make sure you are working in an *open* e-mail.

- **Show Below the Ribbon.** Locate the QuickAccess Bar, which appears at the very top left of your open e-mail. Click on the down-arrow carrot——and select Show Below the Ribbon.

- **Customize QuickAccess Bar.** Click on the down-arrow carrot——again, and select More Commands. A large screen appears. Under Choose Commands From, select All Commands. Scroll down the list in the left column, adding the following list of commands to and removing from the Customize QuickAccess Toolbar column as necessary. You may use the Up and Down arrows to order them to your liking, and then click OK. The recommended list and order are as follows:

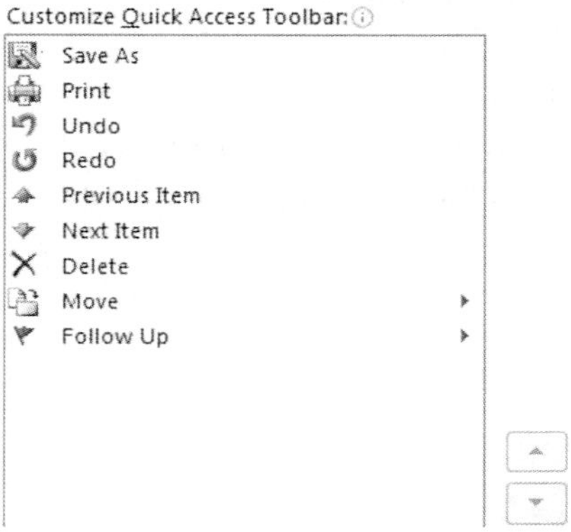

Online Resource: Check out the screencast titled "Setting Up Outlook's QuickAccess Bar" for further assistance at http://www.quietspacing.com/demos.

Exercise—Triaging a Batch of E-mail

With all the Microsoft Outlook settings in place and an explanation of the various onboard tools, it's time to start going through your e-mail. The best way to do this is to identify a small batch of messages—maybe the last ten you've received—to practice your burgeoning QuietSpacing® skills. First, click on the Received column of your Inbox to sort your e-mail from newest on top to oldest on the bottom. Here is the entire series of steps you can take to triage those ten e-mails lickety-quick:

1. Open the first e-mail and identify what QuietSpacing® category it belongs—Trash, Archive, Reference, or Work. (Remember, if you're not sure, ask yourself if anything further needs to be done. If so, it MUST be Work because it's still Open. If not, it MUST be Trash, Archive, or Reference because it's Closed. And as a further reminder, Trash is stuff you will never need again, Archive is stuff you might need again in the distant future as it relates to this particular project/matter, and Reference is stuff you use regularly to perform your Work.)

2. If the e-mail is Trash, click the Delete icon. When you do that, *poof!* the message disappears and the next one in the batch *automatically* opens and is ready to be triaged.

3. If the e-mail is Archive or Reference, click Move to Folder and navigate to the folder where you wish to file it (or create a new one) and click OK. Once again, *poof!* the e-mail is filed and the next message in the batch *automatically* opens and is ready to be categorized.

4. If the e-mail is Work, pause to identify what type of Work it is—an Action Item, Awaiting Response, Pending, or Reading. This helps you manage your workload because your productivity periods are filled with Action Items and Reading, whereas Awaiting Response and Pending are things you only need to monitor.

5. With the type of Work identified, select the red Flag for Follow-up icon and select Custom, then the Due Date (a.k.a. reminder date) you want to be reminded of this Work from the Due Date drop-down calendar. Next, click OK, then the down-arrow icon in the QuickAccess Bar to move to the next e-mail in the batch (or the up arrow if you are moving up your batch).

When you have triaged the entire batch of e-mail, you will be returned to the Inbox. It's that easy.

Now, click on the Due Date column in your Inbox, and all the reminders you set via Flag for Follow-up are arranged by ascending date. (Note: Until you've triaged your entire Inbox, e-mails with no reminders will land on top of those with selected reminders because Microsoft Outlook treats "none" as zero.)

> ➤ **Practice Tip.** Here's a brain bender—cc yourself on **every** e-mail message you send so you can triage your Awaiting Response items. Let's dig down on this one just a bit. One of the key Work items we all track is Awaiting Reponses. These are the items we've completed but are awaiting someone else's input. However, if we just send out e-mails with no way to track when we need to think about them again (a reminder), then we are relying on our memory to make sure that Awaiting Response items don't fall through the cracks. By cc'ing ourselves on the e-mail we send (or at least those to which we need a response), we can set a reminders on them when they return to our Inbox. Then, when the reminder date arrives, the e-mail will queue up for reminder under the Due Date column in the Inbox to remind us to consider whether we've received the response we sought. (Note: You can also do this via the Sent folder in your Inbox. Just find those that you need to track, flag them for follow-up with the reminder date you want to set, and move them to the appropriate folder—either the Inbox or WIP_Awaiting Response.)
>
> Online Resource. Check out the screencast titled "Batch Processing Your E-mail" for further assistance at http://www.quietspacing.com/demos.

DEALING WITH THE BACKLOG OF E-MAIL

Many of you will have quite a number of e-mails stored in your Inbox when you start using QuietSpacing®. There are two ways to triage all your e-mail and reduce your Inbox to just those related to Work (or reduce it to zero if you're a Power User—see below). The first is to slug it out by starting at the bottom and triage everything over the course of time. The benefit of this option is that everything gets properly sorted and handled. The disadvantage is that it can take a long time, depending on the number of e-mails in your Inbox.

The second option is to create a new storage folder with a date-based name, such as As of 1-1-2012. Then sort your Inbox by the Received column. Next, scroll down to the first e-mail you find in the Received column dated January 1, 2012. Click on that e-mail and scroll down to the bottom of your Inbox. Press and hold the Shift key, then click on the last e-mail in your Inbox. This should highlight all the messages between the two you clicked on. Now, drag them all to the new folder you created. This removes them from the Inbox, but they can still be accessed and searched if necessary. The final step of this option is to work through the messages left in your Inbox to get the necessary practice in triaging e-mail so that you can remain in command of your e-mail into the future.

KEEPING YOUR INBOX QUIET—MANAGING TRIAGED E-MAIL

Phew! You've mastered the QuietSpacing® triaging process, and all the e-mail that was in your Inbox has been processed. Of course, that "quiet" Inbox will be displaying new unread e-mail any moment now, plus there are all those flagged Work e-mails awaiting your attention. How do you stay in command of your Inbox now that you've achieved this summit?

There are several disciplines you must adopt to stay on top of the Inbox.

1. **Commit to regular processing intervals—process e-mail in batches.** Start with every fifteen to twenty minutes to keep the batches small and manageable. As your triaging skills mature, you can extend your intervals out to thirty, forty-five, or even sixty minutes. Processing your e-mail in this manner ensures that you are (a) remaining responsive throughout the day, (b) staying abreast of what's going on with the projects you are working on, and (c) minimizing the bouncing around and reactionary behaviors that result from constantly monitoring your Inbox.

2. **Sort your Inbox by Received By and Due Date, depending on what you are doing in your Inbox at this moment.**
Sorting by Received By sets you up for batch processing because it sorts all the unread e-mail to the top. Sorting by Due Date aligns the Work e-mails by reminder date so you know which ones need your attention today. (Note: If you keep your Work e-mails flagged in the Inbox, they will also appear in your To-Do List in the To-Do Bar at the right of your Inbox. This is a nice fail-safe mechanism to ensure you don't forget something.)

3. **Renegotiate flagged Work e-mails that aren't going to get done today.** Renegotiation, as discussed above, is part of the responsibility of being in command of your work. Whenever something that was flagged with a reminder for "today" isn't going to get done—for whatever reason—the Flag for Follow-up Due Date MUST be renegotiated to a future date (Flag for Follow-up, select Custom, select a new Due Date, OK). Failure to do so is a deferral-based behavior and results in your losing command of your workload.

Driving your Inbox through the application of these behaviors and disciplines will keep you highly responsive to those with whom you work, as well as on top of the various responsibilities that constitute your job and career success. The processes described above will assist you in effectively managing your e-mail so you can enjoy the work you do more while reducing the stress this ubiquitous technology can induce.

The To-Do Bar also plays an important role in helping you manage your day. Once it's set up as described above and you've triaged your e-mail, the To-Do List will display those e-mails in the order the reminders were set. As a result, no matter what area of Outlook you are working in, you can glance down at the list to see what else is left for you to attend to today. (Note: The To-Do List is also displayed in Tasks and provides the same assistance. More on that in the chapter titled "Powering through Task Lists" below.)

> ➤ **Practice Tip.** *Another great place to see a collection of e-mail with reminders set is the For Follow-up folder. This is an Outlook system folder found under the Search link in the Navigation Pane of the Inbox. Expand the Search link and click on For Follow-up. Outlook will scan your system to find and place in the folder all e-mail that has a Flag for Follow-up set. Once the search is complete, right-click on the folder and "Add to Favorites." Finally, add the To and Due Date column to this folder (just like we did earlier to the Inbox) so you can sort by Due Date.*

QuietSpacing® E-mail for Power Users

SETUP

If you're ready to go all the way to a *zero* Inbox, then this next section is for you. Note: Most people like to start by keeping all their Open/Work e-mail in the Inbox itself until they are comfortable with the day-to-day application of QuietSpacing® before moving to the zero Inbox. In fact, some people never implement this last step and are very successful with QuietSpacing® because of their ability to sort by Received and Due Date quickly right in the Inbox.

The message here is to come back to these steps once you have worked with QuietSpacing® for a period of time and are comfortable with the day-to-day application of its principles.

- **Create WIP_Folders.** Here's where the fun begins. Our goal is to quiet down your Inbox. To do that, we need to clear your Inbox of clutter—remember, "out of sight, out of mind" is the goal. However, you need to be assured you won't forget anything. That's where WIP_Folders come into play. The WIP—which stands for Work in Process—convention ensures the folders sort together in Outlook's Inbox for easy reference.

  WIP_Folders are Inbox file folders that you create to organize your e-mail-based Work (i.e., stuff that is still in process). Using the types of Work listed in the assessment step discussed earlier,

we'll name the folders according to our Work-status categories—Action Items, Awaiting Response, Pending, and Reading.

> ➤ **Practice Tip:** You will continue to use your regular, preexisting
> storage folders to store electronic Archive and Reference items.

Here are the steps for creating each WIP_Folder:

1. Right-click on Inbox in your Navigation Pane.

2. Select New Folder.

3. Type in the first folder name: WIP_Action Items.

4. Select OK.

5. Repeat for WIP_Awaiting Response, WIP_Pending, and
   WIP_Reading.

6. Now, drag and drop each WIP_Folder up from the All Mail
   Folders area to the Favorite Folders window, and arrange
   them alphabetically. (This only creates a copy of the WIP_
   Folders. The originals are still down below in your All Mail
   Folders area.)

Here's what it should look like when you are finished:

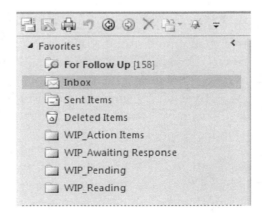

- **Formatting WIP_Folders.** Now, we need to format each WIP_ Folder to display the e-mails stored there in the most effective manner. (Reminder: The next section discusses the specific use of the setup; for now, you just need to get your stored e-mail messages displaying properly.)

1. Click on WIP_Action Items in your Favorite Folders box. As we did above, turn off Show in Groups and Reading Pane. (Refer to instructions above or the QuickStart Card.)

2. Right-click on the horizontal gray bar in the main area of your screen, under WIP_Action Items, for example, next to Subject.

3. Select Field Chooser.

4. Find Due Date.

5. Click and drag Due Date up next to (and left of) Received on the gray bar. (Note: You can use your mouse to resize each column.)

6. Click and drag To up to the right of From.

7. Repeat for each WIP_Folder.

Voilà! Your Outlook Inbox is now set up as a QuietSpacing® Power User. Now, let's look at the additional actions you'll need to master to get to a zero Inbox.

BATCH PROCESSING E-MAIL—INBOX TO ZERO

Follow the same steps listed above under Exercise—Triaging a Batch of E-mail, but add this one step: Once the Flag for Follow-up is set, click the Move to Folder icon to select the WIP_Folder into which you want this e-mail filed. Note, again, that after you make the WIP_Folder selection, the next e-mail in the current batch will open automatically.

Remember, the To-Do List in the To-Do Bar will list all the e-mails you've flagged, arranged by the Due Date you've set. Checking the To-Do List regularly ensures that you are focusing on the reminders you set for yourself. This is a fundamental component in remaining in command of your work, as is the obligation to renegotiate those reminders by the end of the day so that no e-mails are left with "today's" date. That's because you either completed the associated Work or moved the reminder to a future date.

A Final Comment on E-mail

The Inbox has become an invaluable place to communicate and track things you are handling or managing. It's a Grand Central Station of sorts and can be just as busy or quiet as its namesake, depending on the time of day. Staying in command of your Inbox is the best way to continue to be effective in your chosen field. Moreover, as you increase your productivity through leveraging this modern-day tool, you will enjoy a greater sense of success in your career.

QuickTips for Scheduling

- **Schedule time between meetings.** Running from meeting to meeting and conference call to conference call doesn't leave you any time to check in, capture ideas and to-dos, or even just relax and recoup. Try hard-coding a five-minute break between every meeting and call that gets scheduled on your calendar. There's *so* much you can accomplish in five minutes to keep things moving forward. If you find yourself with nothing to push forward, sit down and relax! (Oh, and yes, you'll have to give away a few of those five-minute periods when people ask, but if you never schedule any of them, you won't get any of them at all!)

- **Calendar appointments and task to-dos.** Most of us treat our calendar as a giant melting pot into which we place all our appointments *and* our tasks. The problem with this approach is that the calendar ends up looking like the junk drawer in the kitchen. The brain has to sort through everything, parsing it between hard time (appointments) and soft time (tasks) before getting on with the business of the day. Give your brain a break and put only appointments on the calendar, leaving the tasks for a to-do list—electronic or physical. This frees your brain to do the really hard work of fitting the soft-time demands in between the hard-time demands.

- **Regularly survey all you command.** This old-school notion is also called "taking stock." Our frenetic working worlds have us running from one appointment to a full Inbox, then on to put out the next fire. It seems counterintuitive, but slowing down just a bit makes for faster results. Specifically, at the beginning of each day, take two minutes to review the entire list of demands on your time before launching into that first e-mail. Organize your thoughts and your list around what you expect to get done, communicating any changes to those who need to know. Repeat this exercise at midday—half the day is gone—and again before going home. Not only will you get more done in a timely fashion, but you'll feel more in control, and be more responsive to those who rely on you.

- **Schedule yourself for only four hours a day.** One of the mistakes we all make is overcommitting our time. That's because we think we have eight hours each day in which to get work done. This is not even close to realistic. In fact, we're lucky to get four hours of work time because of all that pops up throughout the day. To the extent that you are able to set deadlines on the work you create or receive from others, schedule yourself for only four hours of productive work time each day. That way you won't spend hours each week requesting or communicating deadline extensions, *and* you'll feel more in control of your workload. And if for some mysterious reason, the emergency du jour doesn't happen, either go home early (!) or get a head start on tomorrow's projects.

- **Establish office hours.** A great way to manage your schedule and work time is to set office hours. These can either be hours you are "available" to others for questions and so on, or hours you are "unavailable" so you can focus on the work you need to do. Either works, but the point is to command the clock just a bit—one or two hours a day—so you can attend to all the work *and* the people who need your time.

- **Take short breaks.** This is a cousin to the *schedule time between meetings* QuickTip, but it's more personal. Numerous brain studies have found that we work best in short bursts (up to ninety minutes). After that, we need some downtime to refresh and renew our mental energy. Throughout the day, find ways to grab a few minutes for yourself. Do a lap around your office (inside or outside). Sit in the reception area and browse through the paper. Take a catnap. These short breaks will reinvigorate you and greatly improve your overall productivity and sense of well-being.

Chapter 4

Effective Scheduling and Productive Meetings

Whenever I watch basketball, I am put in mind of my
clients. Here are these amazing athletes running up
and down court nonstop, dribbling and passing the
ball, watching the shot and game clocks, calling plays,
responding to the coach's directions, and shooting and
rebounding. Doesn't that sound a lot like the modern-day
work environment—running from meeting to conference
call, trying to manage projects, and getting things done,
all while watching the clock to ensure responsiveness?
The only real difference is that most professional
basketball players are getting paid a lot more!

Processing e-mail effectively is the hardest part of QuietSpacing®. The QuickTips for Scheduling above provide some pointers on how best to deal with the day-to-day demands on your schedule. This chapter focuses on how the Calendar function in Outlook can further facilitate your efficiency and productivity.

Preliminary Setup

Those who have attended the seminar associated with this chapter will notice that we cover the material in this guide in a different order. The reason is simple. During the related seminar, we go right from discussing the nature of reminders and how they're used in QuietSpacing® to their technical application in Outlook. Here, we're going to get everything set up properly first, and then discuss specific application of the Calendar function in QuietSpacing®. In the end, the same material is covered in both learning mediums.

Outlook Today Setup

If you skipped chapter 3, "Power-Processing Your E-mail," please return to the beginning of that chapter to get Outlook Today set up and displaying properly.

Once it's set up, Outlook Today is the first screen you see whenever you open Outlook. It lists the events for the next seven calendar days, along with the tasks whose reminders are set for today. This is an electronic way to *survey all you command* (see QuickTips for Scheduling, above) at the outset of your day, as well as renegotiate the reminders for any tasks that aren't going to get your attention today.

To-Do Bar Setup

Again, go to chapter 3, "Power-Processing Your E-mail," to get the To-Do Bar set up and displaying properly if you skipped that chapter. The middle section of the To-Do Bar displays some of your upcoming appointments, giving you immediate visibility into the demands on your time at a glance.

Calendar Setup

Most of us spend the vast majority of our time in our Inbox. That's understandable to a degree since so much of what we do today revolves around e-mail. However, from a different perspective, parking in the Inbox is akin to standing at the end of the driveway, waiting for the mail carrier to arrive. Sort of a ridiculous mental picture, right?

With the Calendar set up properly, including the To-Do Bar, Outlook offers a much more productive location to call Command Central: the Outlook Calendar view. Additionally, getting Command Central set up is relatively simple. The following image displays the QuietSpacing® Command Central setup, with instructions for replicating it below.

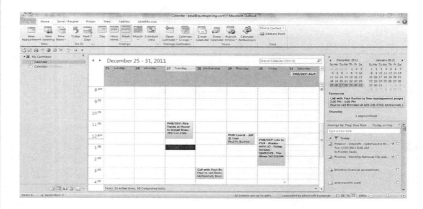

The objective here is to get the best possible dashboard of information at one glance to command our workload. The screen shot above displays seven days of calendar, two thirty-day calendars, a list of upcoming appointments, and all the tasks and e-mails with reminders set for today. That's a tremendous amount of information on one screen!

The basic settings are as follows:

- **Setting a Seven-Day Week.** Select File, then Options. Click on Calendar and confirm that under Work Time the boxes next to all the days of the week (Sun, Mon, and so on) are checked. Click OK.

- **Selecting Week View.** In the Calendar ribbon, in the Arrange section, select Week.

- **To-Do Bar Pane in Normal.** If the To-Do Bar isn't visible, click on the "<" chevron in the top-right area of the Calendar view to display it.

This will give you a vertical seven-day view of your Calendar while also displaying the To-Do Bar.

Here is Command Central.

Online Resource: Check out the screencast titled "Setting Up Command Central" for further assistance at http://www.quietspacing.com/demos.

Integrating Hard-Time and Soft-Time Work

Hard-time work is all work that requires you to be in a specific place doing a specific thing at a specific time. Every appointment on our Calendars is hard-time work. You are required to be someplace—a conference room, an office, on the phone—doing a specific thing—discussing or working on the subject of the appointment. Little else can (or should) be done during hard-time work.

Soft-time work refers to all the other tasks and to-dos that we need to get done. They don't require us to be in a specific place at a specific time. However, they *do* need to be fit into our schedule throughout the day. And that's the rub: when and how to fit all the soft-time work around all the hard-time commitments.

Setting up Command Central facilitates this objective. Humans are visual creatures. We rely on our eyesight as our primary sense. We can use this fact to set up our Calendars to display our hard-time work as visual blocks of time. Then we can remove all the soft-time work from the Calendar itself and place it in Tasks (with reminders) or use Flag for Follow-up on our e-mail so that it all appears in the To-Do List on the To-Do Bar at the bottom right of Command Central. This allows our brain to do the hard work of intermingling the to-dos with the appointments.

Now that we have a reason to use Command Central as our primary view in Outlook, let's look at some of the specific functions in the Outlook Calendar that will help us better manage both the workload and the workflow.

Leveraging the Reminders Window

As discussed in chapter 2, "The QuietSpacing® Architecture," QuietSpacing® is fundamentally a reminder system. Most of us are familiar with Outlook's Reminders Window. It's that annoying box that pops up in the middle of what we're doing to remind us of some appointment or task. Most people immediately reach for their mouse and click on the red *x* in the top-right corner to close it.

STOP DOING THAT!

QuietSpacing® is a *reminder-driven system*. We must learn to ❤ the Reminders Window! Leveraging the functionality of the Reminders Window means we can forget about everything it will remind us of. When we can forget about the future demands on our time, we can focus on the present demands on our time. The result is more focus, which means more gets done and a greater sense of accomplishment.

Now that we're not immediately closing the Reminders Window every time it pops up, let's look at how we can use it to our advantage. The Reminders Window contains four buttons: Dismiss All, Open Item, Dismiss, and Snooze. Here's a quick tutorial on how to leverage these functions in the QuietSpacing® method as they relate to appointments.

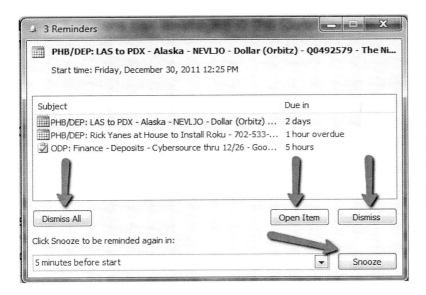

- **Dismiss All.** *Never, ever hit Dismiss All.* The Reminders Window functions just as its name suggests: It reminds us of what needs our attention. Hitting the Dismiss All button *only* removes all items from the Reminders Window. It *does not* mark them Complete or otherwise remove them from our To-Do List or Calendar. A QuietSpacing® best practice is to handle each item in the Reminders Window separately to minimize the risk of user (that's you) error.

- **Open Item.** This is a terrific function, as it allows us to open and *update or renegotiate* anything contained in the item. If an appointment has been rescheduled, we can adjust the start time. If a task or e-mail has a reminder set for today, but it won't get done, we can renegotiate it. We can also change anything in the Subject line or in the Comments area if appropriate. Many Power Users rely heavily on this button to effectively manage their reminders.

- **Dismiss.** For events on the Calendar (such as meetings and tele-conferences), you can use the Dismiss button because either the event took place or it did not. If it was rescheduled, using the Open Item button is a better practice. However, if the event took place or was canceled, a quick click of the Dismiss button will remove it from your Reminders Window.

> ➤ **Practice Tip:** A great way to ensure that everything that re-sulted from an appointment (or meeting or teleconference) has been captured in your QuietSpacing® system is to Dismiss an appoint-ment from the Reminders Window only after all the notes, to-dos, and so on have been recorded elsewhere and reminders for them have been set.

- **Snooze.** The Snooze button is often abused. We tend to pound on it as a way of shutting off the interruption generated by the Reminders Window. However, routinely hitting the Snooze but-ton just creates more self-inflicted interruptions. The only truly valuable use of the Snooze button is if you're being reminded of an appointment in, say, fifteen minutes and you're wrapping up something before prepping for and attending the appoint-ment. A five-minute snooze allows you to finish up the current project while ensuring you don't forget about the impending ap-pointment. If that's not the case, either minimize the Reminders Window or attend to the item you are being reminded about.

Making the Most of Appointments

With the use of the Reminders Window covered, we can focus on the Appointment view itself. Whether we're dealing with a new appointment or an existing one, there are several areas of func-tionality that advance our QuietSpacing® efforts. Generate a new appointment by selecting Calendar from the icon bar on the lower left of the Navigation Pane and click on New Appointment in the upper-right area of the Calendar view.

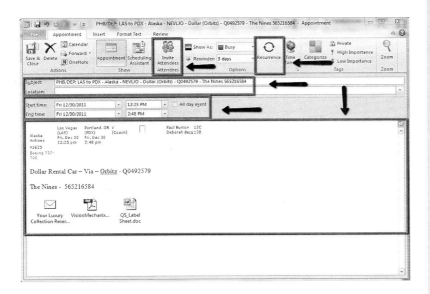

Beginning at the top in the ribbon, there are two functions that make life a lot easier:

- **Invite Attendees.** The ability to invite people to appointments allows you to (a) make sure everyone has the same date/time of the appointment on their Calendar and (b) control what information is contained in that appointment. To use the Invite Attendees function, just select New Appointment, complete the relevant information for the appointment (more on that below), and click Invite Attendees. Add the people's names or e-mail addresses to the To and CC lines, as appropriate, and click Send. Everyone on the list will receive an invitation. (Note: The Invite Attendees function has a host of additional features, but before you explore them, get used to inviting people first.)

- **Recurrence.** Many appointments recur on some regular basis—weekly staff meetings, quarterly board meetings, and so on. You can set them up once on the Calendar, and they will recur until you remove them. Obviously, this is a huge time-saver over setting them up one at a time. As with the Invite Attendees function, select New Appointment, complete the relevant information, and then click on Recurrence. Choose the Recurrence

Pattern and complete the Range of Recurrence per the specifics of this recurring appointment, then click OK. The event will now recur on your Calendar based on the parameters you've set.

- **Subject/Location.** At the risk of repeating what we discussed in the related QuickTips for E-mail before chapter 3, the Subject line is a place where we can, but rarely do, communicate a tremendous amount of information. Whether you adopt a formal naming convention like those displayed below or not, please take advantage of this opportunity to pass along the important information about each appointment (or task or e-mail). In addition, list the location of the appointment (including teleconference bridge information if applicable) so that everyone has the information needed to prepare for and attend in a timely fashion.

Examples of Subject-line naming conventions

Smith/Brown: Strategy Discussion—John Doe—555.333.4444

IBM/20342: Planning Meeting—Annual Retreat—Main Conference Room

- **Reminder engine.** Though its use for appointments is obvious, let's cover the Start Date/Time, End Date/Time, and the Reminder. Whenever you're setting up a new appointment, take care to set the Start Date/Time and End Date/Time correctly. Meeting time is expensive time for organizations, and making a mistake here can be costly if people show up at the wrong date/time, and the appointment has to be reset. Moreover, Outlook (a) automatically checks the Reminder box for all new appointments and (b) defaults that reminder time for fifteen minutes before the Start Date/Time. (Note: You can change that default time in File, Options, Calendar, Calendar Options.)

- **Content collection.** A vastly underused part of Appointments is the content-collection area underneath the Reminder area. It's that blank white space you see in every new appointment. Numerous items can be placed here—Microsoft Outlook files, PDFs, notes from a meeting, and other information that pertains to this appointment. Play with this to see if it's not more expeditious to put *copies* of everything you'll need for or receive from an appointment here, including any notes and to-dos that result. You can always go back to the appointment later to find this information if necessary.

The View from Command Central

Once the Calendar is set up in the QuietSpacing® way, and you have begun to flesh out the information in the appointments you're creating, you'll find that this screen is far more informative than parking in the Inbox, awaiting the next e-mail. Checking your Inbox periodically to triage the latest batch of and/or producing new e-mail means you'll still spend time in the Inbox. However, when you're not actively engaged in e-mail management and production, see if you can get used to sitting in the captain's chair of Command Central.

Making Meetings More Productive

Organizations are made up of people. To be effective, people must meet from time to time to ensure proper alignment. Unfortunately, there tend to be far too many meetings, and many of them are managed poorly. There are entire books on this single subject, making a complete survey of the possibilities for improvement both too long and beyond the scope of this chapter. However, in an effort to ferret out the root cause of why so many meetings are poorly run—and the corresponding waste of time—here are several ideas on how to make your meetings more enjoyable and productive:

- **Reduce meeting length by 25 percent.** Work fills the time allotted—at least that's what the old cliché says. In fact, many of us sit through sixty-minute meetings even though there's no good reason for their being sixty minutes long. The common answer to why we do this is that that's the way it's always been. Try cutting the length of every meeting by about 25 percent: A sixty-minute meeting becomes forty-five minutes, and a thirty-minute meeting becomes twenty-five. The same amount of work will get done, and you've freed up five to fifteen minutes *for everyone sitting in the meeting to do other things!*

- **Require written agendas.** It's difficult to get to a destination if you don't have the directions. Agendas—in particular, written agendas—are the directions for each meeting. Failing to have an agenda is the best way to get lost during a meeting. And remember, meeting time is *the most expensive time the organization and its people have.*

- **State the end time at the beginning.** When the end time for the meeting is given at the beginning, everyone starts on the same page. Moreover, it lets each person in the meeting monitor the time, increasing the likelihood that things will stay on track to result in a productive and timely conclusion.

- **Prohibit PowerPoint.** This may seem blasphemous to many, but PowerPoint is a huge waste of time before and during meetings. Few of us are professional graphic designers. Yet we attempt to use a graphics-oriented software product to reproduce bullet points we could have more easily typed out in Word or—brace yourself—written down on paper and handed out. Similarly, charts and graphics are created in Excel just as easily as they are in PowerPoint. So again, why not just do it there and hand them out? (For those who recoil at the use of paper, remember that most of our electricity is produced with coal-fired generating facilities. Trees grow faster than coal.)

- **Distribute materials the day before.** One of the biggest time-wasters in meetings is having the presenter explain the materials that were handed out at the beginning. The solution is to require that all meeting materials be handed out the day before the meeting. It used to be called homework when we were in the third grade, and there's no reason we can't expect a group of highly paid, competent people to produce, deliver, review, and prepare materials for meetings before showing up. Oh, and there's the fifteen minutes saved …

- **Confirm decisions and action items.** Most meetings are called to discuss matters of serious import, make decisions, and plan action items. A highly effective closing behavior for all meetings is to review—out loud—the decisions that were made and the action items that were assigned, along with anticipated deadlines for those action items. It's a sure way to get everyone on the same page as they exit the meeting.

(Note: This suggestion does not address "status meetings," a.k.a. What-I-Did-Over-My-Summer-Vacation meetings. They should be replaced with status reports that the highly paid, competent team members can read during a quiet moment ... at their desks.)

A Final Word about Effective Schedule Management

This chapter focused heavily on the mechanics of scheduling appointments and running meetings. However, as you turn to the next chapter on task management, be mindful that managing your schedule is fundamentally about managing your time—both the hard time of appointments and the soft time of tasks. Commanding your workload is essentially about mastering this element of QuietSpacing®.

QuickTips for Tasks

- **Do one thing at a time.** Multitasking is neurologically impossible. More and more scientific studies are proving that the brain can do only one thing at time. If you're not convinced, ride as a passenger in a car while the driver is texting. The most productive way to work is to do only one thing at a time. The modern interruption-ridden world is a challenging place in which to attempt this feat. However, any time spent focused on just one thing is more productive time.

- **Identify today's one thing.** Nothing feels quite like crossing things off a to-do list. One way to gain a sense of command over the day and feel good about your day-to-day efforts is to pick one thing on the to-do list each day and commit to getting it accomplished that day. Completing that one thing delivers a palpable sense of accomplishment.

- **Spread priorities out.** Imagine carrying around a sack of bowling balls slung over your shoulder. Each time you utter, "I'll get it done today," imagine placing another bowling ball into the sack. At the end of the day, you carry the sack home to rest at the top of your mind until tomorrow. A great way to lessen that load is to spread priorities out over the course of days and weeks. Almost all deadlines are negotiable, so stop adding to the sack of bowling balls by negotiating longer deadlines.

- **Conduct regular core dumps.** The noisiest place in the world is between the ears. One way to quiet that space down is to write down (or type out) all the "Oh yeahs!" floating around in your mind. Once you've committed them to paper or an electronic to-do list, the only thing to remember is to … wait for it … check the list!

- **Use full screens.** For years now it's been all the rage to have multiple computer monitors in the workspace. Refer to the first QuickTip above. If it's (literally) impossible to do more than one thing at a time, then how can having multiple monitors (or windows open at once) improve your productivity? It can't. Plain and simple. (Note: The only legitimate use of multiple windows or screens is when information from several sources is being aggregated into one place—the "term paper" project, if you will.)

- **Do one more thing.** One of the most simple and effective suggestions for managing tasks and getting more done is to, at the end of each day, do one more (little) thing. Just one. Put a file away. Reply to a quick e-mail or phone call. Jot down a note on a project or to-do. Doing one more (little) thing each day will result in doing approximately 240 more things this year over last!

Chapter 5

Powering through Task Lists

For some twisted psychological reason, it's become a symbol of superiority to expound on how busy we are and how many things we're doing at once. In The Myth of Multitasking, David Crenshaw cites a study by the University of California–Irvine that proves scientifically what we've all known anecdotally for a long time: Multitasking is impossible. Thus, the reality is that we are much more productive (a.k.a. we get things done) when we're focused on one thing. And focus is best achieved when it's quiet both inside our heads and in our surrounding world.

Tasks, projects, to-do lists. These are the indicia of our work-load—the things that must get done. Life (work) would be so easy if we could just arrive at our desks, sit down, and knock out items on the list. But the reality is that e-mail constantly demands our attention, requiring responses and delivering new items for us to do. So too, do the endless meetings and teleconferences we attend. Though this chapter focuses exclusively on the "tasks" function in the quiver of Things Productive, in many ways how we deal with the ever-changing nature of what must be done and when defines how successful we are in managing our time.

Preliminary Setup

Again, those who have attended the seminar associated with this chapter will notice that we cover the material in this guide in a different order. The reason is simple. During the related seminar, we go right from discussing the nature of reminders and how they're used in QuietSpacing® to their technical application in Outlook. Here, we're going to get everything set up properly first, and then discuss specific application of the Task function in QuietSpacing®. In the end, the same material is covered in both learning mediums.

OUTLOOK TODAY SETUP

If you skipped chapter 3—"Power-Processing Your E-mail"—please return to the beginning of that chapter to get Outlook Today set up and displaying properly.

Once it's set up, Outlook Today is the first screen you see whenever you open Outlook. It lists the events for the next seven calendar days into the future, along with the tasks whose reminders are set for today. This is an electronic way to *survey all you command* (see the QuickTip before chapter 4) at the outset of your day, as well as renegotiate the reminders for any tasks that aren't going to get attention today.

TO-DO BAR SETUP

Again, return to chapter 3—"Power-Processing Your E-mail"—to get the To-Do Bar set up and displaying properly if you skipped that chapter. The To-Do List in the To-Do Bar (lower right) displays the task reminders you've set in chronological order, starting with Today. This gives you immediate and ongoing visibility into the demands on your time at a glance.

TASKS/TO-DO LIST SETUP

Before drilling down into the specific setup mechanics for Outlook Tasks, a quick review of new functionality—introduced in Outlook 2007 and refined in Outlook 2010—is in order.

Aside from the introduction of ribbons, which is the most visibly apparent change from Outlook 2003, Microsoft blended its two separate reminder functions into one universal whole. Now, the mechanism for setting reminders for appointments, tasks, and e-mail (via Flag for Follow-up) is the same. This was a long-overdue functionality enhancement that allowed e-mails and tasks to be treat identically.

The reason this is so revolutionary is that it recognizes that many times an *e-mail **is** a task* (or should at least be treated as one) instead of requiring the user to transfer information in an *e-mail **to a*** *task*. This may seem like a small step for Microsoft, but it's a giant leap for how we manage our workload both in Outlook 2010 and in the world at large.

The creation of one universal reminder system allowed Microsoft to create something called the To-Do List. The To-Do List displays anything for which a reminder is set. Therefore, it will list *all* e-mails and *all* tasks that contain any type of reminder. Moreover, the To-Do List can be set to display these items by Due Date (the reminder date in the QuietSpacing® method), meaning that we can see our entire workload, organized by reminder date, in one place at a single glance! And as if that weren't enough, it is displayed both in the Task view and in the bottom right of the To-Do Bar, meaning it's never far away.

So how do we optimize this terrific piece of functionality for QuietSpacing®? First, we need to get the To-Do Bar set up as detailed in chapter 2. Second, we need to get the Task view set up. Here's how:

The objective, once again, is to give us the best possible dashboard of information to command our workload. The key is to strip off what we *don't* need so we can leverage the information we *do* need.

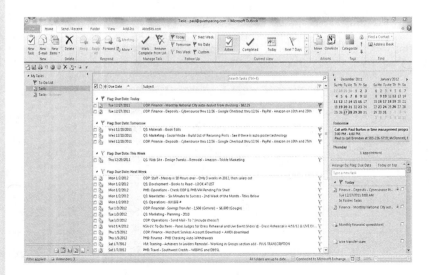

The My Tasks Screen

- Select the Task icon in Outlook to view that screen.
- Click on the Tasks link in the upper-left area of the view.
- Take your cursor and click *and hold* on the Due Date column. Now, drag the Due Date column to the left of Subject.
- Next, click, hold, and drag *off* that row **all** other columns except Sort by: Icon, Sort by: Attachment, Due Date, Subject, and Sort by: Flag Status.
- With the unnecessary columns removed, hover your mouse next to Subject and right-click. In the resulting context menu, select Field Chooser. Scroll down to Complete. Click and drag Complete up to the left-most column and let go.
- Close Field Chooser.

(Note: Confirm that Active is selected in the ribbon under Current View.)

That's all we have to do to get the My Tasks screen displaying the proper information. Note: If you click on the Due Date column, all the tasks will display by Due Date (a.k.a. reminder date) chronologically, which is a terrific way to see what needs doing when. Additionally, if you click the Complete checkbox next to any particular task, it "completes" that task and removes it from the view.

> *Online Resource: Check out the screencast titled "Setting Up Your Outlook Task View" for further assistance at http://www. quietspacing.com/demos.*

Now, let's add to this view the other items (e-mails) for which reminders have been set.

The To-Do List Screen

The setup for the To-Do List screen is virtually identical, with the addition of one new item—the In-Folder column. Specifically:

- Select the Tasks icon in Outlook to view that screen.
- Click on the To-Do List link in the upper-left area of the view.

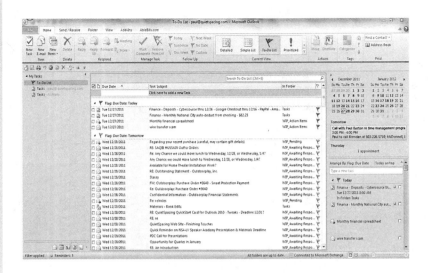

- Take your cursor and click *and hold* on the Due Date column. Now, drag the Due Date column to the left of Task Subject.
- Next, click, hold, and drag *off* that row **all** other columns except Sort by: Icon, Sort by: Attachment, Due Date, Task Subject, and Sort by: Flag Status.
- With the unnecessary columns removed, hover your mouse next to Subject and right-click. In the resulting context menu, select Field Chooser. Scroll down to Complete. Click and drag Complete up to the left-most column, and let go.
- Before closing Field Chooser, select and drag In-Folder up to the right of Task Subject.
- Close Field Chooser.

Again, clicking on the Due Date column arranges all items with a Due Date (a.k.a. reminder date) in chronological order. Also, clicking the Complete checkbox next to a particular To-Do "completes" that item and removes it from the view.

Online Resource: Check out the screencast titled "Setting Up Your Outlook Task View" for further assistance at http://www. quietspacing.com/demos.

Making the Most of the Tasks and To-Do List View

(This section is largely a repeat of the corresponding section in chapter 4—"Effective Scheduling and Productive Meetings." The functionality is very similar, and the decision to repeat it here is in the interest of ensuring a comprehensive discussion in each focal area of the book. There are also some additions to the information that relate specifically to tasks and to-dos, so you are encouraged to review the entire section.)

As discussed in chapter 2—"The QuietSpacing® Architecture"— QuietSpacing® is fundamentally a reminder system. Most of us are familiar with Outlook's Reminders Window. It's that annoying box that pops up in the middle of what we're doing to remind us of some appointment or task. Most people immediately reach for their mouse and click on the red *x* in the top-right corner to close it.

STOP DOING THAT!

QuietSpacing® is a *reminder-driven system*. We must learn to ❤ the Reminders Window! Leveraging the functionality of the Reminders Window means we can forget about everything it will remind us of. When we can forget about the future demands on our time, we can focus on the present demands on our time. The result is more focus, which means more gets done and a greater sense of accomplishment.

Now that we're not immediately closing the Reminders Window every time it pops up, let's look at how we can use it to our advantage. The Reminders Window contains four buttons: Dismiss All, Open Item, Dismiss, and Snooze. Here's a quick tutorial on how to leverage these functions in the QuietSpacing® method as they relate to tasks.

- **Dismiss All.** *Never, ever hit Dismiss All.* The Reminders Window functions just as its name suggests: It reminds us of what needs our attention. Hitting the Dismiss All button *only* removes all items from the Reminders Window. It *does not* mark them Complete or otherwise remove them from our To-Do List or Calendar. A QuietSpacing® best practice is to handle each item in the Reminders Window separately to minimize the risk of user (that's you) error.

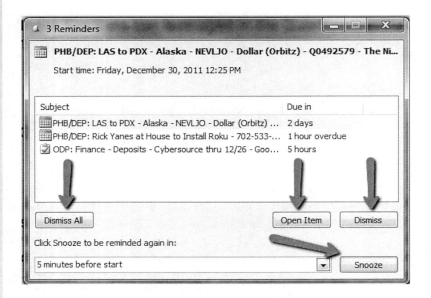

- **Open Item.** This is a terrific function, as it allows us to open and *update or renegotiate* anything contained in the item. If an appointment has been rescheduled, we can adjust the start time. If a task or e-mail has a reminder set for today but it won't get done, we can renegotiate it. We can also change anything in the Subject line or in the Comments area if appropriate. Many Power Users rely heavily on this button to effectively manage their reminders.

- **Dismiss.** Again, dismissing tasks and to-dos from the Reminders Window *only* turns off the reminder. It does not Complete the task or remove it from the Tasks/To-Do List. Therefore, the recommendation is to *never* dismiss a task/to-do from the Reminders Window.

- **Snooze.** The Snooze button is often abused. We tend to pound on it as a way of shutting off the interruption generated by the Reminders Window. However, routinely hitting the Snooze button just creates more self-inflicted interruptions. Stop doing it. Remember, this is the list of things requiring your attention today—*as dictated by you!* Leave everything in your Reminders Window that is set for today and minimize (versus close) the Reminders Window.

> ➤ **Practice Tip:** *One way to rapidly handle completed tasks/ to-dos from the Reminders Window is to right-click on the item to display the context menu. From there, you can select Mark Complete. This will remove it from the Reminders Window and your Tasks/To-Do List views. Note too that you can renegotiate the Due Date from this same context menu by select Follow Up and Custom. Then simply change the Due Date to the new reminder date and click OK.*

Making the Most of Tasks

With the use of the Reminders Window covered, we can focus on the Tasks view itself. Whether we're dealing with a new task or an existing one, there are several areas of functionality that advance our QuietSpacing® efforts.

Start by opening a new task: Select Task from the icon bar on the lower left of the Navigation Pane, and click on New Task in the upper-right area of the Task view.

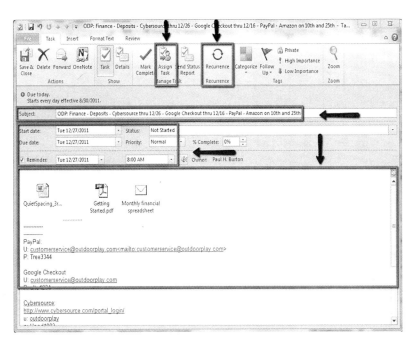

Beginning at the top in the ribbon, there are two functions that make life a lot easier:

- **Assign Task.** Though it is possible to assign tasks to others directly from inside a task (which is similar to inviting attendees to appointments), I don't recommend it. The reason is simple. Recipients are not required to accept the assignment, and if they don't, it will *not* appear on their Tasks list. Moreover, the recipients may not use Outlook Tasks to manage their work, making it unlikely they will see the assigned task even if they accept it.

  However, if your workgroup has a standing agreement to treat Assign Task the same way you treat Invite Attendees, this is a terrific way to assign and track to-dos among group members.

- **Recurrence.** Many tasks recur on some regular basis—weekly reports, year-end activities, and so on. You can set them up once in Tasks, and they will recur until you remove them. Obviously, this is a huge time-saver. To create a recurring task, select New Task, complete the relevant information, and then click on Recurrence. Choose the Recurrence Pattern and complete the Range of Recurrence per the specifics of this recurring task, then click OK. The event will now recur on your Tasks list based on the parameters you've set.

- **Subject.** At the risk of repeating what we discussed in the related QuickTips for E-mail before chapter 3, the Subject line is a place where we can, but rarely do, communicate a tremendous amount of information. Whether you adopt a formal naming convention like those displayed below or not, please take advantage of this opportunity to pass along the important information about each task (or appointment or e-mail).

  Examples of Subject-line naming conventions

  Smith/Brown: Quarterly Project Report—to John Doe—Headquarters

  IBM/20342: Process Billing

- **Reminder engine.** Whenever you're setting up a new task, take care to set the Due Date correctly. Moreover, if you want the task to appear in the Reminders Window, check the box next to Reminder and confirm that it's set for the same date as the Due Date. Note: Always keep the reminder time set for 8:00 a.m. (the default setting). This ensures that *all* tasks with a reminder set for today appear in the Reminders Window first thing in the morning, giving you the ability to *survey all you command* (see QuickTips for Scheduling before chapter 4) at the outset of and throughout the day.

- **Content collection.** A vastly underused part of Tasks is the content-collection area underneath the Reminder area. It's that blank white space you see in every new task. Numerous items can be placed here—Microsoft Outlook files, PDFs, notes from a meeting, and other information that pertains to this task. Play with this to see if it's more expeditious to put *copies* of everything you'll need for or receive from a task here, including any notes and to-dos that result. You can always go back to the task later to find this information if necessary.

But What about the To-Do List?

Noticeably absent from the discussion above is any mention of the To-Do List as it appears in Tasks and in the To-Do Bar. That's because the To-Do List is an amalgamation of tasks and e-mails for which reminders are set using Flag for Follow-up. Consequently, all tasks with reminders will appear in the To-Do List automatically, as will all e-mails that get flagged for follow-up. Handling both of these items is discussed next.

Managing Tasks and/or the To-Do List

In essence, all tasks and to-dos get lumped onto the To-Do Bar. QuietSpacing® relies heavily on the To-Do Bar and, in particular, the To-Do List, to track and queue up all items at the preset (and appropriate) times. Whether the selected Outlook view is Inbox, Calendar, or Tasks, the To-Do Bar—if set to Normal (expanded out into view)—can tell you at a glance what appointments are coming up and what to-dos need attention. Moreover, double-clicking on any item in the To-Do Bar opens that specific item, allowing you to modify information or renegotiate the Due Date (reminder). It really is a powerful tool in the struggle to remain in command of the day while effectively processing everything flowing into the workload.

The key element in this discussion—and throughout the QuietSpacing® method—is the discipline of managing the information flow and the reminders you set. Throughout the day, you *must* periodically review the To-Do List to ensure that what requires your attention today is getting it. Even if your only action is to renegotiate the item to another Due Date, at least you are *taking action* versus deferring action—the second QuietSpacing® principle.

The most effective disciplines for managing the work are to regularly *survey all you command* (see QuickTips for Scheduling before chapter 4), *spread your priorities out* (see QuickTips for Tasks, above), and *conduct regular core dumps* (also in QuickTips for Tasks). Yes, each of these is an administrative effort, but *administration* is just another word for *management*. To *be* in command, you must *act*. In this case, the acts are managerial in nature. Acting periodically throughout the day lessens the burden during each instance and keeps you abreast of the demands on your time. When taking in new tasks, seek to spread priorities out the best you can, and when the noise inside your head gets too loud, get everything down into a captured, static form (e.g., New Task).

> *Online Resource: Check out the screencast titled "Day's End Renegotiation" for further assistance at http://www.quietspacing.com/demos.*

A Final Thought on Managing Tasks and To-Dos

Following the disciplines described above throughout the day makes you more responsive and effective. But *most important,* you must renegotiate everything left on your To-Do List at the end of the day to a future Due Date. Functionally, you finish each day with a clean slate. Failure to do so serves as a reminder of things not done in the past, and what's the value of that? Give yourself the gift of a fighting chance by renegotiating everything to a future Due Date and leave your desk knowing that you have, once again, commanded the day!

QuickTips for Workspaces

- **Create a designated workspace.** One of the most effective ways to increase productivity immediately is to create a designated workspace. Look around your workspace and find a physically definable area—the four corners of your desk, for example—and remove *everything* from it. That includes all the files, piles, pencils, monitors, pictures, phones, and so on. Place one task or project at a time in this designated workspace and focus on what needs to be done on that particular task or project. The result is higher productivity because all those other "things" that used to compete for your attention are now outside your field of vision.

- **Face away from traffic.** One of the worst self-inflicted distractions we create for ourselves is facing the door or opening to our workspace. This means that we glance up each time someone walks by, and if our luck runs out, we make eye contact and in they come. Facing away from this traffic—say, with your shoulder toward the door—produces two results. First, you aren't glancing up anymore, meaning you're not inviting those mini or major interruptions. Second, everyone walking by sees you working! (More on this suggestion in chapter 6.)

- **Sequestering.** Sequestering—hiding away—is something everyone can do to get that one thing done that *must* get done today. Just grab the project and head off to an empty office, a conference room, or the local library. Sit down, work exclusively on those items, and then head back into the fray. Focusing on those few things in a quiet place will result in a more timely and better work product.

- **Elicit versus give answers.** It is often most expedient to quickly answer the questions being asked of you. Unfortunately, this behavior promotes the asking of questions, as opposed to the finding of solutions. Most managers hire their team members to solve problems, not simply raise questions. A best practice for promoting solution finding is to answer questions only with questions. If you help your team members discover the answer for themselves, they'll learn the route to the solution better and take greater ownership of the answer. Think of it as helping them navigate to a new destination as their copilot, letting them drive.

- **Reduce meeting length by 25 percent.** This has already been covered above, but it's so valuable that it's getting a second mention. Meeting time is *the* most expensive time every organization has. Gathering a group of people together all at the same time should be viewed as the greatest opportunity to get things done. Yet many meetings are either unnecessary or inefficient. One of the ways to create more productive meetings and more productive time outside of meetings is to reduce meeting lengths by about 25 percent. That means all sixty-minute meetings are cut to forty-five minutes and all thirty-minute meetings get cut to twenty-five. Then, if we start meetings only at the top of and halfway through the hour, people will (a) be more focused during the meeting period and (b) have a few minutes before the next meeting starts to catch up on and accomplish other things!

- **Distribute materials in advance.** Again, this has already been covered, but it's worth saying again. Another huge time-waster in meetings is handing out the meeting materials at the beginning, and then reviewing what was just handed out. Back in the third grade, we did homework (reviewed materials in advance) so that we could use classroom time to be productive. Where did that notion go? Why are third-graders more productive than adults? Simply stated, if materials are not made available sufficiently in advance of a meeting for people to adequately prepare for and participate in it, then *reschedule the meeting*.

Chapter 6

Maximizing Productivity in the Workspace

Quieting down the physical workspace has amazing effects on productivity. Ironically, just as this is the last substantive chapter of the book, many who adopt QuietSpacing® principles in their workspace do so after implementing the electronic aspects of the methodology. Yet it is the space between our ears and the space in which we work—offices, workstations, and so on—that most often need quieting down to produce the type of environment that allows us to focus on the demands of the day.

The electronic world we inhabit is a mirror image of the physical world. For example, we create and store our work product as "files" in "folders," and we use an "inbox" to collect our e-mail, which is "sent" and "received." Even the icons used to represent these places and actions replicate the physical world. In fact, so much of our work is in electronic form that we can easily forget that the three-dimensional world is where we actually produce the work. This chapter targets the real work world—that of offices and workstations—and seeks to eke out a bit more focus in what is otherwise a frenetic environment.

Physical Operations Setup

Though our world is increasingly electronic, most people continue to maintain physical workspaces and manage mountains of paper and stacks of files. To achieve the goal of increased focus and productivity, we need to organize and set up our physical work area operationally so the QuietSpacing® method will run smoothly.

- **The ergonomics of productivity.** How you organize your office has a lot to do with your efficiency and effectiveness. Yet most of us pay little attention to our ergonomics from a productivity perspective. I routinely walk into what I call the "standard office arrangement," which looks like this:

Standard Arrangement

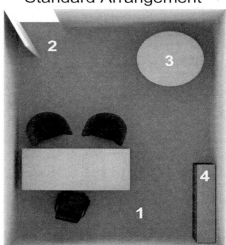

This setup exposes us to several productivity saboteurs:

1. **Closed in.** Our furniture closes us in. It looks and feels tight. Moreover, we have to circumnavigate the entire space to get seated.

2. **Visual interruptions.** An endless parade of distractions passes by the door. Every time we glance up to see who is passing by, it needlessly breaks our concentration. Worse, we might catch someone's eye, prompting him or her to stop and chat for a moment. This seating position creates numerous, unnecessary interruptions.

3. **Unused space/breeding ground.** Whether it's a small conference table, a bookcase, or open floor space, whatever is banished to the far reaches of the room is a breeding ground for piles of clutter—a.k.a. Closed stuff collectors.

4. **Poorly positioned inbox and outbox.** Whether the inbox and outbox are on the credenza or the top of the desk, other people must interrupt us to access them. Moreover, having them directly in our line of sight only heightens our internal noise level by reminding us of what's building up.

Here's an alternative arrangement, the foundation of which works for most people. We can adapt it based on our available furniture and individual needs:

QuietSpacing Arrangement

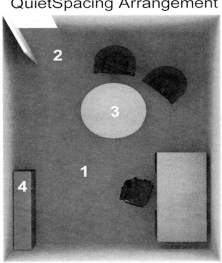

In this arrangement, noticeable improvements are made:

1. **Open and available.** The entire office space is opened up and made available for use. It also feels more flexible.

2. **Distractions and interruptions eliminated.** By not facing the door, we won't be unnecessarily interrupted or distracted. This works both ways. Our eye doesn't catch the movement, and the people passing by see we're working.

3. **Communal working area.** By pulling in a small conference table (or the like), people are welcome into our office to work communally. This area must remain free of stuff. Having this space also eliminates any negative intimation made by our facing away from the door.

4. **Easy in(boxes), easy out(boxes).** Placing the inbox and outbox at the end of the credenza/bookcase nearest the door makes access to them easy for everyone. We can spot-check them on our

way in and out, and others can pop in to do the same without creating large interruptions.

Although these suggestions may seem minor, they work quite well. Just apply a little Adopt, Adapt, Reject. Try this arrangement for a day or two. If it doesn't work, try a different one that seeks to achieve the same result. If neither works, go back to the standard setup, and move on to other parts of QuietSpacing®.

> ➤ **Practice Tip:** For people working in fixed configurations like cubicles, there are lots of ways of implementing these same ideas. Place the inbox and outbox near the space's entry/exit, position the monitor and work areas away from any distractions, and so forth.

- **Setting up your physical workspace.** Even if you don't try a new office configuration, you can still do several things that can improve how you interact with your physical working environment.

  ◦ **Designate one main work area.** As stated in the QuickTips for Workspaces above, the most important part of QuietSpacing® is carving out a quiet space in which to work. More specifically, you must designate a particular location in which you place only the *single piece of work* you want to focus on. This could be your desktop (the whole thing!) or your desk return or computer desk. The only requirement is that you *designate* it as such. This area cannot be bordered by piles (or scatterings) of files you also need to address at some point. It must be devoid of all distraction (i.e., it must be quiet).

  ◦ **Designate one physical inbox and outbox.** The next step is to designate a single area for all incoming physical items and a single area for all outgoing items. This is *not* your entire office! The reason for designating a single area for each is to make it easy to *collect* everything in a manner that minimizes your internal noise (preferably out of your direct line of sight).

❑ **Identify a two-drawer filing cabinet or similar holding area (e.g., bookshelf).** For everything you'll need readily available in the next two weeks, set up a two-drawer filing cabinet (or something similar). You'll use it both during tri-age and during your working day. Each drawer will consist of hanging file folders marked for each day of the week—Monday, Tuesday, and so on. **Place files** and expando folders *between* the daily tabs (either freestanding or in hanging folders of their own—your choice).

❑ Using a filing system of this type allows you to place your miles of piles out of sight. With them out of sight, you can concentrate on what needs doing right now. You won't forget about them because the daily operational process discussed below ensures you are reminded to check the drawers regularly.

> ➤ ***Practice Tip:*** *Many people aren't comfortable with having work hidden away in drawers. Another equally effective setup is a small bookshelf, with each shelf holding a week's worth of work organized by day of the week. Whether the bookshelf has two shelves or five, all the physical work can be organized so that it is quick to use and ensures that nothing is forgotten.*

❑ **Acquire pens and sticky notes (preferably 3 by 5 inches and lined).** Okay, this probably seems too simple, but you'll be surprised at how powerful these tools are in the QuietSpacing® system. You will use them to make notes on top of physical stuff about its disposition.

The Initial Triage Event

The quickest way to learn this part of the workflow architecture and operation of QuietSpacing® is to jump right into an initial pass through your workspace—an initial purge, as it were. Think of this as a spring cleaning. The objective is to take what's already there and pass it through the QuietSpacing® method in an expeditious manner to (a) get it handled and (b) learn through doing how quickly QuietSpacing® can improve your productivity.

This will take a while the first time you do it. How long depends on how backed up your space is. However, experience has shown that it's never as difficult or as lengthy as anticipated. In fact, most first-timers arrive at the end of the initial purge with a sense of wonder ("That didn't take so long!") and relief ("Thank heavens that's done!").

When you're ready to begin, do the following:

- **Capture.** Get EVERYTHING in your office into your physical inbox. If there's too much stuff, expand the size of the inbox. You literally want to clear off all surfaces and spaces that currently serve only as repositories for your stuff. Let's get it all into one place! Oh, and get a big garbage can ready.

> ➤ **Practice Tip.** If, as you clear your physical workspace, you cannot get everything into one place, create definable subsections in your space and tackle one section at a time.

- Triage. Get your pen and sticky notes out, pick up each item, and ask, "What is it?" This question is limited to the following range of answers and related actions:

  ◻ **Trash.** Only things you *know* you need to keep should be saved at this stage. Discard or delete everything else. This is your greatest chance at gaining huge closure.

  ◻ **Archive**. Use your pen and sticky notes to jot down a direction for each item to be archived. Place all physical Archive material into your newly designated outbox. Delegate the archiving effort or designate a date and time on the calendar to do it yourself.

- ❑ **Reference.** Ditto the Archive instructions above, except you must designate an area for the Reference materials to be placed once they are identified. A small reference area in the workspace will do.

- ❑ **Work.** Move through the work-process questions using your pen and sticky notes. The questions and possible answers are as follows:

    - ◆ What type of Work is this? Action Items, Awaiting Response, Pending, or Reading.

    - ◆ When do I need to think about it again? Place each task or project into your two-drawer filing system based on the date you need to be reminded it *exists*. Anything further into the future than two weeks can go into your office's archive system with a similar reminder date set for it to be pulled and returned to you.

When you've cleared the last piece of stuff out of your physical in-box, the initial triage is complete!

The main benefits of conducting the first triage as an all-in plunge are (a) you see and feel immediate benefits from the system and (b) you rapidly get the hang of using the QuietSpacing® methodology.

Though capturing everything is easy—just put EVERYTHING into your inbox—the triage system appears almost too simple on its face. Working through an initial purge demonstrates its effectiveness while ingraining its habits into your psyche.

> ➤ **Practice Tip.** Appendix A offers an alternative method for implementing the QuietSpacing® method based on a multiday schedule, and it applies to both the physical and electronic processes. Some find it easier to Adopt, Adapt, Reject the method when they implement it more slowly.

QuickTips for Mobile Devices

- **The OFF button.** The ability to work whenever you want or need to and wherever you find yourself is fantastic, but it isn't utopian. A fundamental QuietSpacing® objective is increased satisfaction and a greater sense of well-being. The notion of managing your time and your technology is inherent in all pro-ductivity programs. It is your choice whether to *manage* your time and technology or be *enslaved* by it. Make a choice and choose to manage them *both*. What that means in relation to the mobile device is simply this: Remember that it's got an OFF button! Use it when it's appropriate.

- **E-mail: review and clear.** Review and delete e-mail from your portable device during downtimes when you're on the move. Whether you're sitting on the bus during the commute or waiting to board an airplane, run through your e-mail and delete those things you don't need to see again. You'll find that the prospect of having to deal with it again back at your workspace will give you the incentive to increase the number of items you delete.

- **E-mail: brief replies.** The small keyboards of most portable devices do not lend themselves to composing lengthy replies. Amazingly, however, many people persist in attempting to do just that. Strive to use these tools only for quick, concise replies rather than lengthy explanations. If it's that important to pro-vide a detailed answer right now, use the other feature built into the smartphone—the telephone! Even a voice-mail message is better than a cryptic, though lengthy, e-mail.

- **Calendar management.** Two thoughts here. First, learn to make, modify, and cancel appointments on your mobile device. That way you can do it immediately, while in the meeting or during the discussion, instead of having to make a note of it and then deal with it again when you get back to the office. Second, put pertinent information for all scheduled events—such as phone numbers and confirmation numbers—in the Subject line. That means you'll be able to find it easily when you need it.

- **Contacts.** If you are diligent about keeping all your contact information current in Outlook, you will always have it at your disposal via your mobile device. This can save you lots of time when you're on the move.

- **Onboard productivity tools.** Each mobile device has its own specific software packages that come with it or that can be downloaded for free or for a price. Many of these will also facilitate your work during the workday. Learn about these tools and experiment with them, while staying mindful of your organization's policies on these technologies. In the end, tablets and smartphones are better for consumption and communication than production. However, as the technology matures, so too will the ability of apps to deliver powerful productivity options while you're on the move.

Chapter 7

A Day in the Life

Ultimately, the key to success with any productivity method lies in how committed we are to changing our behaviors. QuietSpacing® is no different. QuietSpacing® can change the way you think about information and work, as one client described it. But in the end, you must adopt, adapt, or reject each aspect of the system to customize it to your preferred working environment.

To give you an idea of how all this ties together, let's walk through a day in the life of someone who has implemented many of the suggestions contained in this book.

Arriving at the Office

You arrive at the office and sit down at your desk. You reach over and turn your computer on. As it boots up, you do the following:

- Triage your *single physical inbox*. "What is it?" you ask about each item you find there.

  □ Discard the Trash.

  □ Tag Archive and Reference items with sticky note directives to your assistant.

  □ Further triage. Work through the additional question "When do I need to think about this again?" while you remember to *schedule yourself for only four hours per day* and to *spread priorities out* over a two-week (or longer) period.

- With your *single physical inbox* triaged—something you'll do again *before lunch* and *before going home*—you now take the following steps:

- ❑ Turn to your *two-drawer filing cabinet*, and pull out the Work that was set with reminders for today.

- ❑ Conduct a quick triage on it as well, renegotiating dates for anything that is not likely to get done today given the current state of affairs. The rest is placed near your *designated work area* for quick reference throughout the day.

• Your physical world is ready for production, so remember to employ your noise-reducing tips and tricks throughout the day:

  - ❑ Sequester yourself when necessary.

  - ❑ Set your phone on Do Not Disturb as needed, and apply these rules to your smartphone.

  - ❑ Proactively manage interruptions.

  - ❑ Schedule small breaks.

• Triage your *electronic Inbox*. With your physical world ready, you turn to your computer and open Outlook.

  - ❑ The first screen you see is Outlook Today. Scan your Calendar and Tasks items to determine if anything needs renegotiating.

  - ❑ Click on Tasks and confirm that the To-Do List is displayed. You are presented with something like this:

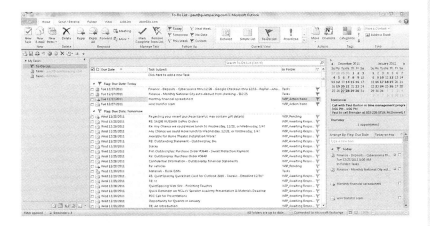

- Work through the items with reminders *set for today*, triaging each one as you go—deleting the Trash, filing the Archive and Reference items, keeping some of the Work on the To-Do List for today, or renegotiating the rest of the Work to a future date. The rest you can disregard for now.

▫ Now that you have briefed yourself about what's on your plate, click on your Inbox to see the e-mails that arrived overnight. If your Inbox was at zero when you stopped working last night, there's only so much to triage. If you are still working on getting to zero, focus on the new e-mails that came in overnight. You'll get to the others as time permits.

- Starting at one end of your Inbox, triage e-mail and file it accordingly.

- Delete Trash.

- Move Archive and Reference items to your electronic filing system.

- Mark Work items with Flag for Follow-up and either leave them in the Inbox or, if you've moved to Power User status, move them to the appropriate WIP_Folder.

> **Practice Tip:** *Remember, a quick way to file your Work e-mail is to use the Move to Folder icon in the ribbon. Once you've flagged an e-mail, click on Move to Folder and select the folder where you want that e-mail to be filed. Outlook places the e-mail in that folder and opens the next e-mail. Note: You'll notice that the folders you use the most appear at the top of the list. To find other folders, simply select the Move to Folders option at the bottom of this screen and navigate to the folder you need.*

▫ Click on your Calendar view (Command Central) to see what the rest of the day and week hold for you.

- ☐ Review your Reminders Window and the To-Do Bar through-out the day to keep on track with what you have queued up.

- At day's end. By day's end, all reminders must be completed or re-negotiated to another day. The same is true for your physical files.

The more you incorporate these tips and tricks into the workflow system, the more noise you eliminate. This will directly increase your focus and corresponding productivity. The net result is higher accomplishment and greater career satisfaction.

Conclusion

Even keeping things simple can take time and pages in a guide such as this. The QuietSpacing® workflow-management system is nonetheless straightforward. The suggestions surrounding its ar-chitecture are derived from numerous client implementations, which time and time again have proved that we really *can* make positive changes to significantly improve our productivity and work lives. A critical key is remembering to apply the three tenets discussed at the beginning of the program:

(1) Productivity is about focus.
(2) Stop deferring; start deciding.
(3) Adopt, Adapt, Reject.

Then, just mix in some optimism and commitment to change, and you will succeed. Your productivity, responsiveness, and effective-ness will all improve. You will feel more in command of your career and more accomplished in your life.

Final question: What are you going to do with your three days?

Appendix A

Five-Day
Implementation Schedule

Many clients don't think they have the time to implement QuietSpacing® all at once. In fact, many are skeptical about the program's benefits and want to see some smaller successes before launching into full-scale adoption. Both are reasonable responses, which is why the program can be implemented using a more gradual method.

The following is a five-day schedule that allows you to ease into QuietSpacing®'s concepts and processes. Of course, each step may take more or less than a day, but the idea here is to give you a step-by-step mechanism for success. Because we are spreading out the implementation, we'll tackle a little bit of the physical stuff and a little bit of the electronic stuff each day.

DAY ONE	
Physical Stuff	Electronic Stuff
Designate a Workspace	Clear Computer Desktop
Identify one central working area in your office. This will become the place where you will place only one thing at a time. Thus, it must be devoid of all other stuff. To prepare this area, conduct a triage on all the stuff that is captured there. (Revisit, if necessary, the instructions in the chapter 6 on how to conduct a physical triage.) This space, once cleared, must remain clear of stuff *except* what you are currently working on. Simply triage your Work to another area in your office for temporary storage. Day Two clears these items into a more organized system. (Of course, Trash is thrown away, Archive items are filed away, and Reference items are put away.)	Turn on your computer to the initial screen (past your login). This is the desktop. Just as we did for your designated workspace, conduct a triage on your computer desktop to eliminate all the unnecessary shortcuts and icons on the screen. Move shortcuts you use often to the Quick Launch Bar down next to Start. Delete all others. You can use the Start function for those less frequently accessed items. File all other documents on the desktop in their appropriate Archive or Reference folders. If an item is Work, open an Outlook Task and move (drag and drop) it into the Task, craft a descriptive Subject line, and set a Reminder.

DAY TWO	
Physical Stuff	Electronic Stuff
Establish Multi-Drawer/ Shelf Filing System	Set Up General Outlook Inbox Setup
To quiet your space down, you need a place to put all the stuff stacked about your workspace. But you also need to be assured you won't forget it.	Work through the setup steps in chapter 3 that affect the general settings you want Outlook to have. Specifically:
Some people use a two-drawer (or more) filing cabinet. Some prefer to use a multi-shelf bookshelf because they'll be able to at least still *see* their stuff.	• Outlook Today • To-Do Bar • QuickAccess Bar
Use hanging files or dividers on each shelf or in drawer to designate the five days of the week. There should be a five-day divider set for each drawer/shelf you use.	• Inbox – Turn off Show In Groups – Turn off Reading Pane
Place the Work materials from Day One into their appropriate place— in/on the drawer/shelf of the week and behind the divider for the day of that week you want to be reminded of this Work stuff.	– Turn off AutoPreview – Open Next/Previous Item
Note: You'll be doing the same thing for the other stuff you triage in the rest of your office when we get to that step.	– Turn off New E-mail Notification – Insert To and Due Date columns

DAY THREE	
Physical Stuff	Electronic Stuff
Identify Single Inbox/Outbox	Set Up Outlook Calendar and Tasks
Another key to effectively using the QuietSpacing® method is to minimize the number of ways you can be (and allow yourself to be) interrupted. Establishing a single place in your workspace for inbound stuff and outbound stuff facilitates that goal. The size of the single inbox and/or outbox is irrelevant. Make them as big as you want, as long as they don't become your entire working environment! The only location recommendations are that they not be right in front of you or near your designated work area. The big change here is cultivating the discipline of use them. This means encouraging other to use them (mandating, if possible) and using them yourself. *Any* time something comes into your work world or leaves it, it needs to pass through the inbox/outbox areas. This includes things you bring into your workspace yourself, preventing you from placing them right in the middle of your designated work area or some other "unauthorized" area for untriaged stuff!	Work through the setup steps in chapters 4 and 5 that affect the settings you want Outlook to have as it relates to the following: • Calendar • Tasks

DAY FOUR	
Physical Stuff	Electronic Stuff
Clear All Surfaces, Then Drawers of Stuff	Set Up Outlook Inbox WIP_Folders
Now that you have the hang of triaging your physical stuff, it's time to work through your entire office. This process can take some time, so there are two distinct ways of reaching this goal: 1. Set aside several hours of quiet time (possibly a weekend or other after-hour period) and dig into the task with a fury. You'll find that most of the stuff in your working environment is Closed stuff—Trash, Archive, and Reference. When you are finished, the physical setup for QuietSpacing® will be complete. 2. Identify segments of your workspace that you can attack over time. Though it will take longer to complete, you won't have to set aside a significant period of time to accomplish the task. Note: Make sure to assemble all the tools you'll need before getting started on each method—trash can, sticky notes, paper, writing instruments, manila folders.	Work through the setup steps in at the end of chapter 3 for e-mail Power Users that affect the settings you want your Inbox to have as it relates to the WIP_Folders.

DAY FIVE	
Physical Stuff	Electronic Stuff
Adopting/Adapting to the System	Migrating to a Zero Inbox
Most people find things about the physical methodology that work very well for them. They also need to adapt and disregard other elements to fit the overall QuietSpacing® scheme into an effective model for their work styles and working environments. My ongoing advice to everyone is to do the best they can to memorize the QuietSpacing® tenets and architecture. With those readily available, adapting the methods becomes easy and highly productive.	A zero Inbox seems out of reach for most clients when they first start working with QuietSpacing®. Remember, it's just a massive triage that you can do over time. Once you have optimized Outlook to facilitate your success, the only thing left is your commitment to reaching the goal and staying there. Here are a couple of thoughts to keep in mind while winnowing down that enormous mountain of e-mail: 1. Life flows like a river. It's a natural, normal, and, to be candid, reassuring fact of life. One consequence of this fact is that backsliding and recovery happen. It's all about the discipline of success and your desire to achieve it. 2. The underlying benefit of a reminder system is to move the future into the future so that you can focus on today's stuff today. 3. Renegotiating reminders is a successful use of QuietSpacing®'s powerful methodology. You are actually succeeding at *not* forgetting things by using the reminders and flags in Outlook.

A play-by-play analysis of each day looks something like this:

Day One: Two things are accomplished here. First, you achieve clear progress. You now have a designated work area and computer desktop that are *much* quieter than what you had in the past. Second, you have begun triaging successfully. The triage process is one of the core skill sets in QuietSpacing®, and the ability to immediately begin perfecting yours goes a long way toward achieving success with it.

Day Two: Day Two lines you up to begin implementing the various facets of QuietSpacing® that work together to achieve your overall goals.

Day Three: You continue getting ready for the big push in Day Three by setting up the final components for the physical workspace and getting the supporting characters in Outlook—Calendar and Tasks—set up properly.

Day Four: With the triaging skill well practiced, Day Four sees the start of the major initiative to clear the working area of all the historical stuff that can be better stored elsewhere. Completing this step provides a huge visible benefit to your psyche and announces to those around you that you're back in charge of your workload! On the electronic side, you complete the setup processes in preparation for a similar push on the Inbox.

Day Five: Applying your new disciplines is the watchword for Day Five and beyond in the physical world. Maintaining a semblance of perspective and understanding your role in making your own work/life satisfying will greatly assist you in maintaining diligence with your newfound methods. Having seen the results from your work in the physical world, you now turn to your Inbox with the skills to conquer your e-mail. You work through the backlog as time allows or as you mandate, never forgetting the underlying tenets of flow and focus.

Congratulations! You're now well poised to begin taking advantage of what QuietSpacing® offers in terms of increasing your productivity, effectiveness, and results! But remember Tenet Three: Adopt, Adapt, Reject. Making the most of QuietSpacing® is really about molding the methodology to your existing work routines and preferences.